Discussion Strategies

Beyond Everyday Conversation

Second Edition

David Kehe
Peggy Dustin Kehe

Illustrations by Andrew Toos

PRⓄ LⓘNGUA
LEARNING

Pro Lingua Learning

PO Box 4467
Rockville, MD 20849 USA
Office: 301-424-8900
Orders: 800-888-4741
Web: www.ProLinguaLearning.com
Email: Info@ProLinguaLearning.com

At Pro Lingua Learning,
our objective is to foster an approach
to learning and teaching that we call
interplay, *the **inter**action of language*
learners and teachers with their materials,
with the language and culture,
and with each other in active, creative,
*and productive **play**.*

The topics in this book were gathered from articles in a variety of newspapers: *The New York Times, The Los Angeles Times, The Seattle Times, The Seattle Post-Intelligencer, The Chicago Tribune, The European, The Observer, The Japan Times, The Daily Yomiuri,* and *The Stevens Point (Wisconsin) Journal.* All of the illustrations are by Andrew Toos except for the cartoons used with news articles on pages 37, 50, 62, 115, 154, and 174 which are clip art from the *Art Explosion 250,000 Images* collection © 1997 by Nova Development Corporation and the photographs from Dreamstime.com: p. 181 © Viorel Sima, p. 192 © Suzanne Tucker, p. 196 © Stuart Corlett, p. 198 © Lbarn, p. 200 © Monika Adamczyk, p. 207 Koscusko, p. 209 © Lisa F. Young, and p. 210 © Monkey Business Images.

This book was designed and set by Arthur A. Burrows using Century Schoolbook for the text and display type. It was printed and bound by Sheridan Books, Inc. in Ann Arbor, Michigan.

Second edition.

Introduction

These activities follow and build upon the strategic conversation skills of our intermediate-level book, *Conversation Strategies*. However, this text stands on its own and may easily be used for its own purpose: developing discussion skills. The activities in *Discussion Strategies* are designed to help high-intermediate to advanced level ESOL students develop the skills needed at high levels of communicative interaction.

From the early units on, students, in a step-by-step procedure, are given extensive practice in a variety of discussion strategies for leading and participating in a discussion. They are given focused practice with the following discussion techniques:

- using rejoinders
- asking follow-up questions
- seeking and giving clarification
- using comprehension checks
- answering with details
- soliciting more details from others
- interrupting others during a discussion
- recounting something they have heard
- volunteering an answer
- helping the leader of a discussion
- expressing an opinion
- referring to a source when giving an opinion
- leading a discussion themselves

Each unit builds on and recycles the strategies practiced in the previous ones, and for that reason, it is recommended that the class proceed through the book unit-by-unit in the given sequence. By the final units, students, while discussing sophisticated topics, are using all the strategies in large-group or whole-class situations.

Introduction

The general progression of interaction formats in the book is from participating with a partner in pair-work to leading large-group discussions. In the table of contents the interaction formats are indicated as pairs, triads, small groups, and large groups or whole class.

In many of the units, summaries of newspaper articles are used as the topics for practicing the strategies and for carrying out the discussion. These articles have been chosen for their high-interest content. No article requires in-depth background knowledge, and the topics can be discussed by students from any culture.

> ## To students and teachers:
> ## **All the articles in this book are true stories.**

CONTENTS

General Structure of the Book

Discussion Strategies by Unit

* The number followed by a letter – 67B, for example – indicates the page number and Student A, B, C, D, or E.

Contents

Contents

Contents

Contents

Discussion Strategies

A Note of the General Structure of the Book

All of the activities in this book are for discussion groups. The first twenty-eight units, those which introduce and provide controlled practice of the discussion strategies, are for groups of two to five students. Units twenty-nine through thirty-nine, starting on page 191, give the students an opportunity to use their new strategies in less structured discussions; they involve large groups or the whole class in open discussion of the articles provided.

For the first twenty-eight units, each student has information not to be shared with other students except as part of the discussion activity. To help make this clear to the students, they are called Students A and B in pair activities, A, B, and C in triad activities, etc. And the book is divided into sections, the first for Student A, the next for Student B starting in page 67, and the third for Student C (and where appropriate Students D and E) starting on page 133. These sections can be found easily using the black tabs marked AAA, BBB, and CCC, as you can see on the facing page. For example, Unit 1 begins on page 1 for A, page 67 for B, and page 133 for C.

We don't want anyone to get lost, so let's be sure everyone is on the right page and then start off with Unit 1. Have fun.

Rejoinders	Follow-up Questions
I see.	*(Questions about an answer)*
Oh, yeah?	**A: What did you do last night?**
Really?	**B: I watched a movie on TV.**
That's great!	A: *(Rejoinder and Follow-up)* **I see.**
That's too bad.	<u>**What**</u> **movie did you watch?**

A
A
A
A
A
A

Format: Triads – Student B, page 67; Student C, page 133

Before the discussion
(1) *Silently* complete the questions below.
(2) Write two more questions about any topic.

Discussion Directions
(1) Ask *both* of your partners your discussion questions.
(2) After they answer, ask **follow-up questions** and use **rejoinders**.
(3) Take turns. You begin with discussion question #1. Student B asks #2, then Student C asks #3, and you continue.
(4) Answer your partners' questions *with details*.

Discussion Questions
1. Did you _____ yesterday?

4. When you were in high school, did you ever _____ ?

7. Have you ever _____?

10. What are some good points about _____ ?

13. Was anyone in your family ever a victim of a crime (e.g.,robbed by a thief)? *[Note: "e.g." is an academic abbreviation meaning "for example."]*

16. Which would you prefer to visit, a museum, a park, or a zoo?

19. _____ ?

22. _____ ?

Note: Follow-up questions frequently use WH-questions.
What movie?	Where did you see it?
Who was in it?	Why did you choose that one?
What did you think of it?	How long was it?
How often do you go to the movies?	

Clarification Expressions

A
A
A
A
A
A

Pardon? **Excuse me,** }}	**What/Who/Where did you say _____ is?** **Did you say _____?** **You said _____, right?** **You did what?** **I'm afraid I didn't understand that.**

Format: Pairs – Student B, page 68

Before Part 1 of the discussion
   Without talking to your partner, fill in the blanks in Part 1.

Part 1 *Note: When two choices are given in parenthesies, choose one. Example, (yes/no)*
   (1) Read your sentences to your partner and respond to their
      clarification expressions.
   (2) Try to have a brief discussion about the topic in each sentence.

   1. I'm planning to buy _____ this year.
   2. Some day, I'd like to meet _____.
   3. The movie I think you should see is _____.
   4. _____ is a big problem.
   5. Could you help me? I need help with _____.
   6. _____ is one of the most interesting people in this school.
   7. When I was a child, I spent a lot of time _____.
   8. There are three things (my friend /I) really hate(s): _____.
   9. If I had only one month left to live, I would _____.
  10. (My friend / I) did something (funny / embarrassing) once. Here's
      what happened: _____.

Part 2
   (1) Listen to your partner. Using **clarification expressions**, ask
      for clarification *after each sentence*, even if you understand clearly.
   (2) After your partner answers, ask *follow-up questions* (see Unit 1)
      in order to have a brief discussion about the topic in each sentence.

   1. *After sentence 1, ask:* Excuse me, you want to work in a *what* ?
   2. You said you think computers are _____, right?
   3-10. (Ask for **clarification** after each sentence.)

Clarification Questions, I
Comprehension Checks

> **(Do you) understand _____?**
> **OK?   (Have you) got it?**

Focus: Sentence-by-sentence clarifications with questions provided
Format: Pairs – Student B, page 69
Topics: Part 1. Flight Attendant Hero
            Part 2. Lost in a Jungle

Before Part 1 of the discussion
  (1) *Silently* read your article in Part 1.
  (2) Write answers to the *Factual Questions* about the article.

Part 1
  (1) Read this article to your partner.
  (2) *Stop after each sentence* and ask your **comprehension check.**
  (3) In response, your partner will ask a **clarification question**.
  (4) When you have finished all the sentences, ask your partner
      the *Factual Questions* and *Reaction Questions.*

Flight Attendant Hero

1. This article is about a 31-year-old flight attendant.
      Do you understand this first sentence?
2. The flight attendant works for British Airways.
      Understand sentence 2?
3. She was on a flight over the Atlantic Ocean on the way from
   London to New York.
      Do you understand this third sentence?
4. As the plane was flying over the ocean, the flight attendant
   looked out the window and saw some black smoke on the water.
      Got it?
5. It was very cloudy, but for about 20 seconds it was clear, so she was
   able to see the smoke.
      Understand sentence 5? *The article is continued on the next page.*

Clarification Questions, I   **• 3**

A
A
A
A
A
A
A

6. Flight attendants are trained to report anything unusual, so she told the pilot about the smoke on the water.
   OK?
7. The pilot turned on the emergency channel of his radio, and he could hear a signal from a fishing boat saying it needed help.
   Got the seventh sentence?
8. The pilot called the police in Boston, and they sent a ship to rescue the fishermen on the boat.
   OK?
9. Also, there was a helicopter in the area taking pictures of whales. They heard the pilot's call and rescued the fishermen.
   Do you understand what I just said?

Factual Questions about the article

Ask your partner the following questions.

1. What airline did the flight attendant work for?

   _____

2. Where was the plane flying to?

   _____

3. Was it a sunny day or a cloudy day?

   _____

4. What did the flight attendant see out the window?

   _____

5. What did the pilot do after the flight attendant told him about the smoke?

   _____

6. Who rescued the fishing boat?

   _____

Unit 3 is continued on the next page.

Clarification Questions, I

Reaction Questions about your partner's opinions and experiences. Ask these questions and ask some follow-up questions.

1. What airlines have you flown on?
2. When you fly in a plane, do you usually feel nervous?
3. Have you ever wanted to be a pilot or a flight attendant?
4. Have you ever seen an accident?
5. Have you ever gone swimming, fishing, or sailing on an ocean?

(You think of some *Reaction Questions* about this topic.)

6. _____

7. _____

Part 2

(1) Listen to your partner read a news article.
(2) *After each sentence,* your partner will ask a **comprehension check**. In response, ask one of the **clarification questions** below. There are nine sentences.
(3) Then answer the *Factual Questions* and *Reaction Questions.*

Clarification Questions

Lost in a Jungle

1. Did you say it took place in North America?
2. What did you say was in the middle of the rain forest?
3. What sickness did the uncle get? And could you spell it?
4. Why did they eat wild fruit?
5. Could you repeat that, please?
6. You said that there were snakes, crocodiles, and what?
7. Did the jaguar kill them?
8. I didn't understand that. Could you repeat it?
9. What did they have on their bodies?

Factual Questions about the article
Answer your partner's questions.

Reaction Questions about your opinions and experiences
Try to answer all your partner's questions and follow-up questions *with details.*

Clarification Questions, I   • 5

Clarification Questions, II

Focus: Sentence-by-sentence clarifications, questions *not* provided
Format: Pairs – Student B, page 72
Topics: Part 1. Giant Baby
Part 2. Music, Reading, and Math

Before Part 1 of the discussion
(1) *Silently* read your article in Part 1.
(2) Write answers to the *Factual Questions* about the article.

Part 1
(1) Read this article to your partner.
(2) *Stop after each sentence* and ask your **comprehension check.**
(3) In response, your partner will ask a **clarification question**.
(4) When you have finished all the sentences, ask your partner the *Factual Questions* and *Reaction Questions*.

Giant Baby

1. There is a 17-month-old baby named Zack who is very large.
   Do you understand this first sentence?
2. Even though he is only a baby, he is about 1 meter tall and weighs 31 kilograms, which is about the size of an eight- or nine-year-old child.
   Did you understand that?
3. Because he is so large, he has to wear diapers that are adult size.
   Got it?
4. Also, he has to go barefoot because regular baby shoes don't fit him.
   OK?
5. Zack comes from a large family: his mother is 180 cm. tall and weighs 100 kilos; his father is 190 cm. tall.
   Do you understand what I just said?
6. Zack's mother was worried that he had a disease that made him so large, so his doctors did some special tests, but they found no physical problems.
   Understand?

This newspaper story is continued on the next page.

---

7. His mother is also worried because sometimes people are cruel to people who are different.
   Got it?
8. People often stare at Zack when he goes shopping with his mother, but, except for that, people have been very kind and helpful.
   OK?
9. Recently, some people gave Zack's parents an extra-large stroller for him and a special seat to use in the car.
   Understand?

A
A
A
A
A
A

Factual Questions about the article

Ask your partner the following questions.

1. How old is Zack? (a) 12 months (b) 17 months (c) 24 months?
   _____

2. Is he bigger or smaller than most children who are his age?
   _____

3. What does he wear that's adult size?
   _____

4. Why does he go barefoot?
   _____

5. Who's taller, his mother or his father?
   _____

6. Why did the doctors do some special tests on Zack?
   _____

7. What do people do when they see Zack at the supermarket?
   _____

8. What did some people give Zack's parents?
   _____

Unit 4 is continued on the next page.

Reaction Questions about your partner's opinions and experiences. Ask these questions and ask follow-up questions.

Giant Baby

1. When you were a baby, were you bigger or smaller than average?
2. Who is the largest person in your family?
3. Do you like your size now? Do you wish you were bigger? Or smaller?
4. Describe the size of the person you would like to marry.
5. Would you like to have children some day?
6. Tell me about a baby you recently touched, held, or played with.
7. What do you think is the most difficult thing about babies?
8. Tell me about an experience you had when people stared at you.

Part 2

(1) Listen to your partner read a news article.
(2) *After each sentence,* your partner will ask a **comprehension check.** In response, ask a **clarification question.** Samples are given below. *Even if you understand clearly,* ask a clarification question for practice.

Sample Clarification Questions

Did you say _____?
Could you explain what a _____ is?
Why did _____?
How many _____?
Who/What/Where/When/Why did you say _____?
I'm afraid I didn't understand that. Could you repeat it?

Factual Questions about the article
Answer your partner's questions.

Reaction Questions about your opinions and experiences
Try to answer your partner's questions *with details.*

Clarification Questions, II

Answering with Details

Format: Triads – Student B, page 75; Student C, page 134

Before the discussion
(1) *Silently* read and answer the questions below for yourself, but *do not write the answers*.
(2) Write two more questions about any topic.

Discussion directions
(1) Ask these questions of *both* of your partners.
(2) After they answer, ask them follow-up questions.
(3) Answer their questions *with details* by using **and, but, so, because,** or **two sentences** each time you answer.

Discussion Questions

Some Personal Questions

1. Are you happy now?
4. After getting married, what would cause you to divorce your spouse?
7. Do you often use the internet?
10. What is your opinion of *this* group's members?
13. Do your parents treat you and your siblings equally?
16. What is one environmental problem in your country?
19. _____?
22. _____?

Discussion

Discussion

A
A
A
A
A
A
A

Format: Triads – Student B, page 77; Student C, page 135
Topic: Your High School Days

Before the discussion
  (1) **Silently** read the questions below, but **do not write** the answers.
  (2) Write two more questions about the topic.

Discussion directions
  (1) Ask these questions of *both* of your partners.
  (2) After they answer, ask them **follow-up questions**, and use **rejoinders** (e.g. "I see," "That's too bad," or "That's great!").
  (3) Also, answer your partners' questions *with details*.

Discussion Questions:

Your High School Days
1. How did you get to school every day?
4. How long did it take you to get to school every day?
7. Did you belong to any clubs? If so, how many days a week did you have club activities?
10. About how many close friends did you have?
13. Did your school allow students to have part-time jobs?
16. In general, were you satisfied with your school rules?
19. Did your school have computers for students to use?
22. Were your high school days happy or boring for you, in general?
25. How many people from your high school days do you still keep in contact with?
28. Did you prefer to have male teachers or female teachers?
31. About how many hours a day did you study outside of school?
34. What is your happiest memory from your high school days?
37. _____
40. _____

Paragraph Clarifications, I

A
A
A
A
A
A

Focus: Paragraph-by-paragraph clarifications, with clarification
 questions provided
Format: Triads – Student B, page 78; Student C, page 137
Topic: Animals in Movies

Before Part 1 of the discussion

(1) *Silently* read your part (A) of the article about animals in
 movies in Part 1.
(2) Write the answers to the *Factual Questions* about the article
 in Part 4.

Part 1

(1) Read this first part of the story (A) to your partners.
(2) *Stop after each paragraph* to ask your **comprehension check.**
(3) Then answer your partners' **clarification questions.**

Animals in Movies (A)

1. Have you ever seen a movie in which an animal was hurt or killed?
 Do you think this was a cruel thing to do to an animal?
 Do you understand this first paragraph?

2. There is an organization called "The American Humane Society"
 (in other words, AHS). This organization makes sure no animals
 are hurt or killed in movies. Before AHS started, many animals
 were hurt or killed during movie-making.
 Any questions about paragraph 2?

3. The first time an animal was hurt in a movie happened in a cowboy
 movie in 1939. In that movie, a specially-trained actor rode his
 horse off a mountain cliff and jumped into a river. The actor was
 OK, but the horse died. Many people were angry about this, so,
 after that, the AHS became advisors to movie-makers.
 Understand paragraph 3?

Unit 7 is continued on the next page.

Parts 2 & 3

Listen to Students B & C tell their parts of the story. *After each paragraph*, ask the **appropriate clarification question** below.

PARAGRAPH 4: Can you explain what a "battle" is?
PARAGRAPH 5: I'm afraid I didn't understand what you said.
PARAGRAPH 6: Did you say elephants jumped out of the airplane? Were they killed?
PARAGRAPH 7: You said the animals feel stress. Why?
PARAGRAPH 8: How many fish did they need?
PARAGRAPH 9: Could you explain that again?

Part 4

Factual Questions about the story
Ask your partners the following questions.

1. What is the abbreviation (in other words, the initials) for "The American Humane Society"?

_____

2. What is the job of the AHS?

_____

3. What happened in the cowboy movie in 1939?

_____

4. Why were people angry about this cowboy movie?

_____

Reaction Questions about your partners' opinions and experiences. Ask these questions and ask follow-up questions.

You, Animals, and the Movies

1. Tell me about a movie you saw recently that had an animal in it.
4. Do you go to movies often?
7. What is your favorite type of movie? Action? Mystery? Romance? Horror?
10. (You think of some questions about this topic of movies and animals.)

A
A
A
A
A
A
A

Paragraph Clarifications, II

Focus: Paragraph-by-paragraph clarifications, clarification
questions *not* provided
Format: Triads – Student B, page 80; Student C, page 139
Topic: Sleep

Before Part 1 of the discussion
(1) *Silently* read your part (A) of the article about sleep in Part 1.
(2) Write the answers to the *Factual Questions* about the article.

Part 1
(1) Read this first part of the story to your partners.
(2) *Stop after each paragraph* to ask your **comprehension check.**
(3) Answer your partners' **clarification questions.**
(4) Then ask your partners your *Factual Questions.*

Sleep (A)

1. Researchers are studying sleep. Research shows that people
   generally have two sleepy times every day: first, in the afternoon,
   around 2 to 4 p.m., and then around 10 p.m. to midnight.
   Do you understand the first paragraph?
2. Do you understand the expression "a sleep-deprived person"? A
   sleep-deprived person is someone who doesn't get enough sleep;
   in other words, they need more sleep than they get. Research
   shows that a normal person will take 10 to 15 minutes to fall asleep,
   but a sleep-deprived person will fall asleep in 3 or 4 minutes.
   Understand?
3. If you get sleepy after eating a big dinner, or while listening to
   a speech or concert, or after drinking a little alcohol, then you are
   sleep-deprived. If you can't stay awake all day without drinking
   some coffee or tea, then you are probably sleep-deprived.
   Got it?

Unit 8 is continued on the next page.

Factual Questions about the article

1. How many sleepy times are there every day for most people?

   _____

2. What are the sleepy times?

   _____

3. What does the expression "a sleep-deprived person" mean?

   _____

4. How long does it take a normal person to fall asleep?

   _____

5. How long does it take a sleep-deprived person to fall asleep?

   _____

6. What are three habits that show that you are sleep-deprived?

   _____

A A A A A A

Parts 2 & 3

(1) Listen to your partners read the rest of the article.
(2) When they ask if you understand, ask your own
clarification questions, *even if you understand clearly.*

Part 4

Reaction Questions about your partners' opinions and experiences. Ask these questions and ask follow-up questions.

Sleeping Habits

1. How many hours sleep do you need to feel good?
4. How many hours a night did you sleep when you were in high school?
7. Do you usually sleep better if you've gotten exercise during the day?
10. If you only sleep two or three hours at night, do you have problems the next day? (For example, do you feel irritable or unfriendly?)
13. (Think of two more questions about **sleep** and ask your partners.)

Asking for More Details

A
A
A
A
A
A

> **Could you give me an example of** _____?
> **What do you mean by** _____?
> **Could you explain** _____?
> **Could you tell me why/who/what** _____?
> **I'd like to know more about** _____.

Format: Triads – Student B, page 82; Student C, page 141

Before the discussion
   Silently read the sentences below and fill in the blanks.

Discussion directions
   (1) Read these sentences to your partners.
   (2) Listen to your partners' sentences. **Ask them for more details**.

Discussion Starters

   1. My best friend _____

   _____

   4. If I could have one thing that would improve my life, it would be

   _____

   _____

   7. The thing I'm most afraid of these days is _____

   _____

   10. One thing I'd like to change about the world is _____

   _____

   13. In my opinion, the students in this class _____

   _____

   16. I once told a lie about _____

   _____

Discussion

Format: Triads – Student B, page 83; Student C, page 142
Topic: Stress

Before Part 1 of the discussion
  (1) *Silently* read your part (A) of the article about stress in Part 1.
  (2) Write answers to the *Factual Questions* and then write two
      more questions.

Part 1
  (1) Read this first part of the article (A) to your partners.
  (2) Answer any clarification questions they have.
  (3) Ask them your *Factual Questions*.

Stress (A)

This is an article about stress. According to research, people who are close to their friends and family tend to live longer than loners. **Do you understand "loners"?** And people who have had heart attacks will live longer if they have close friends and family members.

To get more information about stress, researchers studied 40 monkeys. First, they put the monkeys in 4 groups. **Understand?** Then they shifted 3 or 4 monkeys from one group to another. For monkeys, it is very stressful to join a new group. So researchers could study the effect of stress on the health of the monkeys. **Have you got that?** They found that some monkeys remained friendly with each other even in stressful situations. For example, the friendly monkeys touched each other, combed each other's hair, and sat near each other. **OK?** After 26 months, they found that the friendliest monkeys were the healthiest. Also, the monkeys who were aggressive and upset from stress had the poorest health. **Do you understand this first part?**

Unit 10 is continued on the next page.

The friendliest monkeys were the healthiest

Discussion

Factual Questions about the article

1. Who lives longer, people with many friends, or loners?

_____

2. How many groups of monkeys were there in the research project?

_____

3.

_____

4.

_____

A
A
A
A
A
A

Parts 2 & 3

(1) Listen to your partners read the second and third parts
of the article.
(2) Ask clarification questions when you don't understand.
(3) Answer the *Factual Questions* they ask you.

Part 4

**Reaction Questions about your partners' opinions and
experiences.** Ask the questions below and ask follow-up questions.
Also, answer your partners' questions with details.

Stress in Our Lives

1. Do you have a friend or family member that you feel very
   close to? Who?
4. If you feel stress, do you: (a) eat food and candy (b) talk to a
   friend (c) go shopping (d) do some exercises (e) drink alcohol
   (f) do meditation to clear your mind (g) other?

(Think of two more *Reaction Questions*.)

THE CHILDHOOD HOME
MATCH THE HOUSE WITH THE FACE

A.

B.

C.

D.

E.

F.

Discussion

Discussion

Format: Triads – Student B, page 87; Student C, page 145
Topic: Your Hometown and Childhood Home

Before the discussion
(1) ***Silently*** read the discussion questions below, but ***do not write*** the answers.
(2) Write two more questions about the topic of your hometown and childhood home.

Discussion directions
(1) Ask *both of* your partners your discussion questions.
(2) Also, try to use these *discussion strategies*.

── Discussion Strategies ──

Ask **follow-up questions** and **solicit more details.**
  (e.g., "Could you give me an example?" "What do you
  mean _____?" or "Could you explain _____?")
Use **rejoinders.**
  (e.g., "I see," "That's too bad," or "That's great!")
Answer questions **with details.**
  (e.g., answer with *and, but, so, because,* or with *two sentences*)

Discussion Questions

Your Hometown and Childhood Home

1. Where is your hometown?
4. When you were in junior high or high school, did you want to have a different hometown?
7. Do you have to worry about bad weather conditions like floods, tsunamis, typhoons, or snow storms in your hometown?
10. **Now let's talk about our childhood homes.** What was your favorite room in your childhood home?
13. Did you share your bedroom with anyone?
16. What view could you see outside your bedroom windows?
19. _____
22. _____

Discussion   **• 21**

Student A • Unit 12 ⌒◡◡

┌─ Interrupting Someone ─┐

Excuse me. Could I ask something?
Uhh, sorry for interrupting, but . . .
Excuse me, but I have a question.

A
A
A
A
A
A

Format: Triads – Student B, page 88; Student C, page 146
Topic: Telling Lies

Before Part 1 of the discussion
(1) **Silently** read your part (A) of the article about telling lies
   in Part 1.
(2) Write answers to your *Factual Questions* about the article.

Part 1
(1) Read this first part of the article (A) to your partners.
(2) ***Don't ask them if they understand***, but answer their
   clarification questions when they interrupt you.
(3) When you're finished, ask them your *Factual Questions*.

Telling Lies (A)

Most people would probably say that they hate it when someone lies to them. However, telling small lies, called fibs, is common. For example, have you ever told a friend that his or her hair style looks good, when actually, you thought it looked terrible? This is an example of a fib.

Researchers did a study on lying and found that lies are a part of everyday life. For instance, sometimes students will tell a lie in order to get a better grade, or a worker will tell the boss a lie in order to get a promotion. However, those are not the most common type of lies. More often, people lie in order to get other people to respect them. For example, let's say you exercise 4 days a week for about 40 minutes. If you want to impress a friend, you might tell him, "I exercise almost every day by jogging or by playing tennis for one hour." You didn't really tell the truth; you told this little lie because it made you feel good about yourself. This is the most common type of lie.

Unit 12 is continued on the next page.

Interrupting Someone

Factual Questions about the article

1. What are fibs?

   _____

2. What is an example of a fib?

   _____

3. When a worker tells a lie in order to get a promotion, is this the most common type of lie?

   _____

4. Why would someone lie to a friend about how many minutes they exercise?

   _____

5. Is lying to make you feel good about yourself a common or uncommon reason to lie?

   _____

Part 2

   (1)   Listen to Student B read the second part of the article.
   (2)   Interrupt *while* Student B is reading and ask **some clarification questions** *even if you understand clearly.*
   (3)   Try to use the **"Interrupting Someone"** expressions.

   For example: Excuse me. Could I ask something? What is the first type of lie called?

Part 3

   Listen to Student C, interrupt, and ask clarification questions.

   For example: Uhh, sorry for interrupting, but did you say introverts tell more lies?

Unit 12 is continued on the next page.

A
A
A
A
A
A

Part 4

Reaction Questions about your partners' opinions and experiences. Ask these questions and follow-up questions.

To Lie or Not to Lie

1. Let's say you're planning to go to a restaurant with your friend. Your friend says that he wants to eat at a Chinese restaurant, but you don't really want to eat there. If your friend said, "Is it OK with you if we eat at a Chinese restaurant?" would you tell the truth? Or would you lie and say, "Good idea. I want to eat there too"?

4. If someone asks you how much you weigh, do you tell the truth?

7. Tell me about a lie that you told your parents, a teacher, or a friend, when you were younger.

10. Do you think people in your country are usually honest or do they often tell polite lies? Give me some examples.

Words That Describe

┌─────────────── **Expressions** ───────────────┐

It is a person/animal/place/thing that ____.
It is an event/condition/situation that _____.
It is a type/kind/sort of ____.
You can find it at/in ____.

└──┘

Format: Triads – Student B, page 91; Student C, page 149

Before starting
(1) *Silently* look at the words in the list below.
(2) *Do not show or tell your words to your partners.*

Directions
(1) Take turns. Using the expressions above, describe your
    words to your partners.
(2) Don't say the word.
(3) Your partners will try to guess the word.
(4) If they cannot guess the word, they can ask a question.

snake	crime	introvert	river
diapers	email	Youtube	festival
stress	parachute	toy	a lie
	coeducational school		

Dropping a butter knife during a meal means a male visitor is forthcoming

Discussion

Discussion

Format: Triads – Student B, page 93; Student C, page 151
Topic: Superstitions

Before Part 1 of the discussion
(1) *Silently* read your part of the article (A) in Part 1 below.
(2) Write answers to the *Factual Questions* and write two
    more questions.

Part 1
(1) Read this first part of the article to your partners.
(2) Then ask your *Factual Questions*.

Superstitions (A)

Galina is a 26-year-old Russian woman. When she gets out of
bed every morning, she tries to touch the floor with her right
foot first in order to avoid bad luck. If she had a bad dream
during the night, she will turn on the water in the bathroom
and retell the dream to the running water so that the bad
dream will disappear down the drain. Also, during a meal, if
she drops her butter knife, she believes she will have a male
visitor. If she puts on her sweater or shirt inside out, she takes
it off, throws it on the floor, and steps on it before putting it on
the right way. **Do you understand so far?**

Russians have always been very superstitious, especially
about important events such as marriage, death, and traveling.
One custom is called "sitting for the road." Before starting a
trip, everyone sits together for a moment in silence on their
suitcases, a couch, or a bed. This custom is followed by
traveling businessmen, diplomats, and even cosmonauts.
Do you know what a cosmonaut is?

Unit 14 is continued on the next page.

Factual Questions about the article

A
A
A
A
A
A
A

1. According to the Russian woman, which foot should touch the floor first in the morning?

_____

2. What does the Russian woman do if she has a bad dream?

_____

3. _____

4. _____

Parts 2 & 3

   (1) Listen to your partners read the second and third parts of the article.
   (2) Interrupt and ask clarification questions when you don't understand.
   (3) Answer your partners' *Factual Questions*.

Part 4

Reaction Questions about your partners' opinions and experiences

   (1) Ask these questions and then follow up-questions.
   (2) Answer your partners' questions with details.

It's Your Lucky Day

1. What are some traditional things that people in your country do for *good* luck?
4. Do you have a lucky number?

(Think of two more *Reaction Questions* about superstitions.)

Telling What You've Heard

┌─── **Phrases for Telling** ───┐

A told me about . . . .
B said (that) . . . .
C told me (that) . . . .
B explained (that) . . . .
According to A, ...

Format: Triads – Student B, page 95; Student C, page 153
Topics: Part 1. Short People Live Longer
Part 2. Gossiping
Part 3. Why the French Have Fewer Heart Attacks

Before Part 1 of the discussion

(1) *Silently* read your article in Part 1.
(2) Write the answers to the *Factual Questions* about the article.

Part 1

(1) Tell Student B about your article, "Short People."
(2) Do *not* tell Student C.
(3) Student B will tell C what they heard about the article.
(4) Ask Student C your *Factual Questions* below.

Short People Live Longer

Researchers have found that short people seem to live longer than
tall or heavy people. The researchers studied 400 men and found that
shorter men lived about five years longer than taller men. Also, they
found that smaller dogs, horses, and mice tend to live longer.

The researchers explained the reason for this. There are chemicals in
the body called hormones. Certain hormones cause a person's body to
become large. However, these same hormones also cause the body

This article is continued on the next page.

A
A
A
A
A
A

to get old faster. In a certain kind of very tiny mouse, they found that smaller individuals did *not* produce three types of hormones, or chemicals, that larger mice produce. As a result, the small mice of this species lived a year longer than the larger ones.

This research is especially important, because some doctors give special hormones to small children in order to help them grow larger. Unfortunately, these same hormones may cause the children to die younger.

Factual Questions about the article "Short People Live Longer"

1. Who lived longer: short or tall people?

_____

2. Is this true or false? Smaller dogs live longer than bigger ones.

_____

3. How many years longer did short men live than tall men?

_____

4. What do we call the chemicals in our bodies that make us grow larger?

_____

5. What do these same hormones also cause our bodies to do?

_____

6. Which type of mouse had the three types of hormones: the large or small ones?

_____

Part 2

(1) Leave your group and sit in a different part of the room. *Do not listen* to Student B's article.

(2) After Student B tells Student C about the article, come back to the group. Student C will explain the article to you.

(3) Answer Student B's *Factual Questions* about the article.

Unit 15 is continued on the next page.

Telling What You've Heard

Part 3

  (1) Listen to Student C tell you about the article, "Vegetables and Wine." **Don't take notes.**

  (2) Tell Student B about the article.

  (3) Student B will answer Student C's *Factual Questions* about the article. **Don't answer or help.**

Part 4

Reaction Questions about your partners' opinions and experiences. Discussion about the article, "Short People Live Longer"

Your Feelings about Size

1. Are you happy with your height, or do you wish you were shorter or taller?

2. Are your family members tall, average, or short?

3. In general, have your relatives lived to an old age?

4. Do you think you will live to an old age?

5. If you had a child that was very short, would you ask a doctor to give them hormones to make them bigger?

Volunteering an Answer

⌐ Phrases for Volunteering ¬

I think (that) . . .
In my opinion, . . .
I'd like to say (that) . . .
May I say (that) . . . ?
Can I answer that?
Can I respond to that?

Format: Small Groups – Student B, page 98; C, D, E 156-158

Directions for Asking

(1) Ask your questions below in any order.

(2) ***Do not ask anyone directly*** (In other words, don't look at anyone or say anyone's name.)

(3) Your partners will volunteer to answer.

Directions for Volunteering

(1) ***Volunteer to answer*** your partners' questions ***with details***.
(Answer with **and, but, so, because,** or **two sentences**.)

(2) Try to answer first sometimes, and sometimes wait for your partners to volunteer.

(3) Ask follow-up questions, too.

Questions for volunteers to answer

- What time do you usually get up?
- Who did you talk to on a cell phone today?
- Have you ever smoked a cigarette?
- Can I find your picture on the internet?
- How much money do you think you have with you right now?
- (You think of some questions.)

Discussion

Format: Triads – Student B, page 99; Student C, page 159
Topic: Divorce

Part 1

Pre-discussion

    (1) Before starting this discussion on divorce in Europe, ask
       your partners these questions.
    (2) Answer their questions.

1. This article is about divorce in Europe. Do you think divorce
   rates there are increasing or decreasing? What do you think is
   the reason for this?
4. Among European women, what do you think is the average age
   for marriage: (a) 18 (b) 23 (c) 25 (d) 28?

Part 2

Discussion Directions

    (1) Read the first part of the article to your partners.
    (2) Listen to Student B read the second part of the article.
    (3) Listen to Student C read the third part of the article.

DIVORCE (A)

The rate of European divorces has been increasing recently. This is especially true in the northern countries,
where the number of divorces rose between 1960 and 1992.

While the divorce rate increased in *all* the countries, it was
lower in countries that are traditionally Catholic. **Do you
understand "Catholic"?** For example, the divorce rate
was lower in Spain, Italy, Portugal, and Greece. On the
other hand, Britain, France, and the Scandinavian countries
had higher divorce rates. In fact, Britain had the highest
divorce rate, with one divorce in every three marriages.

This article is continued on the next page.

HEY! WHERE'S THE CANDLES?.. WE USED TO HAVE CANDLES EVERY NIGHT ... are you listening to me?

Many Young People feel it is important to have a Romantic Relationship ...... They expect to have a perfect marriage

There are several reasons why divorce is increasing. First, women are becoming more financially independent. In other words, it is easier nowadays for them to find good-paying jobs, so they don't have to depend on husbands to support them. For example, in Scandinavia, where women are very independent, there tends to be a higher divorce rate. Second, many young people feel it is important to have a *romantic* relationship with their spouse. In other words, they expect to have a perfect marriage. However, if the marriage is not like their dreams, they start to look for a new and better spouse.

A
A
A
A
A
A

Part 3

Factual Questions about the article
Read the questions in *Part 1* to your partners again and try to answer their questions.

Part 4

Reaction Questions about your partners' opinions and experiences

Your Feelings about Marriage and Divorce

1. Is the divorce rate in your country increasing? If so, what are the reasons?
4. Do you think love is necessary in order to have a good marriage?
7. In your country, is it common for a couple to live together before marriage?

Student A • Unit 18 ～～
Clarifying by Summarizing, I

A
A
A
A
A
A

Focus: Summarizing (clarifications are provided)
Format: **Pairs** – Student B, page 102
Topics: Part 1. Getting Fat
                        Wrong Stadium
          Part 2. Bugs in Manila
                        Naked in the Laundromat

Before Part 1 of the discussion
   (1) *Silently* read your two articles in Part 1.
   (2) Write answers to the *Factual Questions* about the articles.

Part 1
   (1) Read these two articles to your partner.
   (2) *After each article,* answer your partner's **summary
       clarification questions**.
   (3) Then ask your *Factual Questions* and *Reaction Questions*.

Getting Fat

I'm going to tell you about two articles. The first article
is about Africa. There is a certain tribe in one country
who thinks that fat people are beautiful. The men in this
tribe think women are more attracted to fat men than
to thin men, so many men try to become fatter. **Did you
understand these first sentences?** Women think that if
a man has a fat stomach, it means he is rich and can buy a
lot of food. **Understand?** In fact, every October, the tribe
has a contest to see who is the fattest man. To become fatter
and to win the contest, one man lay in bed for 12 weeks and
drank 19 liters of milk every day. **Did you get the third
part?**

Unit 18 continues on the next page

Clarifying by Summarizing, I

Wrong Stadium

The second article is about two high schools in the U.S.
They were scheduled to have a football game against each
other. At the start of the game, an airplane was supposed
to fly above the football stadium and two men were supposed to jump out of the plane and parachute onto the
middle of the football field. **Did you understand this
first part?** Unfortunately, the airplane pilot, who was
a beginner, got lost. After a while, he saw a football stadium, so the men parachuted out of the plane. However, it
was the wrong stadium. **Did you get the second part?**
Some people in this wrong stadium, who were watching
the football game there, thought the men coming down in
parachutes were terrorists. Meanwhile, the people at the
other game kept watching the sky and waiting for the airplane with the men in parachutes to arrive. **Understand?**

Unit 18 continues on the next page

Factual Questions about the articles

A
A
A
A
A
A
A

1. In the first article, where did the story about fat men take place?

   _____

2. Why do the men try to become fatter?

   _____

   _____

3. What do women think when they see a fat man?

   _____

   _____

4. Why did that one man drink 19 liters of milk a day?

   _____

5. In the second article, why did the men jump into the wrong stadium?

   _____

   _____

6. What did the people in the stadium think when they saw the men coming down in the parachutes?

   _____

Reaction Questions about your partner's opinions and experiences. Ask these questions and ask follow-up questions.

Two Articles

1. Which do you think is more attractive, someone a little fat or someone a little skinny?
2. If you wanted to gain some weight, what would you do? What if you wanted to lose weight?
3. Tell me about a contest you or a family member has been in.
4. Which would you rather do, jump out of a plane with a parachute, climb a dangerous mountain, or go deep-sea diving with air tanks on your back?
5. When were you recently watching something as a member of an audience?

Unit 18 continues on the next page.

Clarifying by Summarizing, I

Part 2

(1) Listen to your partner read two articles.

(2) *After each article*, ask these **summary clarification questions**.

(3) Then answer your partner's *Factual Questions* and *Reaction Questions*.

A
A
A
A
A
A

Summary Clarification Questions

About the first article

1. I think you said that there is a problem in Manila because people are making fires and cooking roasts, right?
2. So if someone has a lot of cockroaches in their house, they can pay the police to kill the insects and they have to pay the police 10 cents for every dead cockroach?
3. In other words, a person with a roach farm can raise a lot of cockroaches and sell them to the government. Is that right?

About the second article

1. You said the man was alone in the laundromat because it was early in the morning, right?
2. I'm not sure if I understand. Did you say the man didn't want to take off his clothes because it was too cold, so he wore his wet clothes in the dryer?
3. I think you said the woman called the police when she saw the man. Did she call them because he was naked?

Factual Questions about your partner's articles

Answer your partner's questions.

Reaction Questions about your opinions and experiences

Try to answer your partner's questions *with details*.

Clarifying by Summarizing, II

A
A
A
A
A
A

Focus: Summarizing (clarifications are not provided)
Format: Triads – Student B, page 105; Student C, page 162
Topic: Catching Colds

Before Part 1 of the discussion
(1) *Silently* read this first part of the article (A) in Part 1.
(2) Write answers to the *Factual Questions* in Part 4.

Part 1
(1) Read this first part of the article to your partners.
(2) Answer their **summary clarification questions**.

Catching Colds (A)

In fall and winter, many people catch colds. In fact, colds are the most common reasons people miss work or school. People spend billions of dollars on cold medicines, but many people do not understand how we catch colds. **Did you understand this first paragraph?**

These are ways people do NOT catch colds: We don't catch colds because the weather suddenly changes or because cold air blows on us. Also, we do NOT catch colds because we didn't wear a hat when it was cold outside or because we went outside with a wet head. Also, we do NOT catch colds from too much work or from staying up late at night. **Understand?**

You may be surprised to learn that you can kiss someone with a cold and NOT have to worry that you'll catch it. Also, you do NOT have to worry if someone with a cold sneezes or coughs on you; in fact, we do NOT catch colds from people sneezing on us. **Got it?**

Unit 19 is continued on the next page.

Clarifying by Summarizing, II

Parts 2 & 3

    (1) Listen to your partners read the rest of the article on colds.

    (2) Ask **summary clarification questions** when asked if you understand, *even if you do understand clearly.*

    (3) Use the following expressions.

A
A
A
A
A
A

Summary Clarification Questions

Did you say _____?   You mean _____?

You said _____, right?   In other words, _____, right?

I think you said _____, right?

I'm not sure I understand. Did you say _____?

Part 4

Factual Questions about the article

    Ask these questions and answer your partners'.

    1. What's the most common reason people miss work or school?

    _____

    4. In winter, if you take a bath and then go outside with wet hair, will you probably catch a cold?

    _____

    7. If your brother has a cold and he sneezes on you, will you probably catch his cold?

    _____

Reaction Questions about your partners' opinions and experiences. Ask these questions and then ask follow-up questions.

You and the Common Cold

    1. Before you heard the information in this article, how did you think people caught colds?

    4. What are some traditional cures for a cold in your country?

    7. What do you usually do to keep healthy?

Telling Other People's
Opinions and Experiences

A
A
A
A
A
A

Format: Small Groups – B, page 107; C, page 164; D, page 166

Part 1
   (1) Discuss the *topics* below with your partners.
   (2) Try to give details and ask questions to get more details.
   (3) Listen closely to what your partners say, because in Part 2
      you will tell new groups what they said.

Discussion topics
   1. Tell us about a foreign country you've visited.
   5. Tell us about a terrible or an embarrassing experience you've
      had.

Expressions for Telling
Others' Opinions and Experiences

I don't have an opinion about that,
      but I know someone who . . .
I haven't, but _____ has.
            (friend's name)

I've never done that, but my friend . . .
I'm not sure, but someone told me . . .
I don't know, but I do know someone who . . .

Part 2
   (1) Get into new groups.
   (2) Ask your new partners the questions below. Answer
      their questions by telling what you learned in your first
      group in Part 1. Use the expressions for "Telling Others'
      Opinions and Experiences."
   (3) ***Do not tell your own opinions or experiences***.
   (4) Ask questions to get more details.

Unit 20 continues on the next page.

Discussion questions

1. Have you visited any foreign countries?
5. Have you had any terrible or embarrassing experiences?

Part 3

(1) Discuss the *topics* below with your partners.
(2) Try to give details and ask questions to get more details.
(3) Listen closely to what your partners say, because in Part 4 you will form a new group and tell what they said.

More discussion topics

1. Tell us about a strange relative you have (e.g., a brother, uncle, or cousin).
5. Tell us about the most money you spent in one day or during one weekend.

Part 4

Directions

(1) Get into new groups again.
(2) Ask your new partners the questions below and answer their questions. Tell what you learned in your second group in Part 3. Use the expressions for "Telling Others' Opinions and Experiences."
(3) ***Do not give your own opinions or experiences.***
(4) Ask questions to get more details.

More discussion questions

1. Do you have any strange relatives?
5. Have you ever spent a lot of money in one day or during a weekend?

Discussion

A A A A A A

Format: **Triads** – Student B, page 109; Student C, page 168
Topic: Driving

Before Part 1 of the discussion

(1) *Silently* read your article about driving in Part 1.
(2) Write answers to your *Factual Questions* and write two
    more questions.
(3) Write two more *Reaction Questions* in Part 4.

Part 1

(1) Read this first article to your partners.
(2) Then ask your *Factual Questions.*

Driver Goes to Prison

A driver who was drunk hit another car with his pickup
truck and killed two college students. This accident
happened in North Carolina, where the law says a
drunk driver can be punished by death if they kill
someone. Lawyers wanted the driver to get the death
penalty because they wanted to make him an example
for other people who might try to drive after drinking.
In other words, people might not drink and drive if they
know they could get the death penalty. In the end,
the drunk driver was sentenced to spend the rest of his
life in prison.

Unit 21 is continued on the next page.

Factual Questions about your article

Ask your partners these questions.

1. What was the drunk man driving?

_____

2. How many college students were killed?

_____

3. _____

4. _____

Parts 2 & 3

(1) Listen to your partners read the second and third articles.
(2) Interrupt to ask them clarification questions when you don't understand.
(3) Answer their *Factual Questions*.

Part 4

Reaction Questions about your partners' opinions and experiences

Ask these reaction questions and some follow-up questions. Write two more questions to ask. Answer your partners' questions with details.

Dealing with Drunk Drivers

1. How do you think drunk drivers should be punished if they kill someone while driving?

2. Does your country have strict rules about drivers who drink?

3. _____

4. _____

Helping the Discussion Leader Explain, I

Format: **Triads** – Student B, page 112; Student C, page 171

Expressions

Could you help me explain that?
Do you know what I mean?

Example

A: When I got up this morning, I felt irritable.
B: What do you mean by "irritable"?
A (to Student C):   Could you help me explain that?
C (to Student B):   Sure. He means he was in a bad mood.
He was cross, grumpy, and mad at the world when
he got up this morning.

Part 1

(1) Read the following sentences to Student B.
(2) Student B will ask you to clarify, but **you don't clarify.**
(3) Ask Student C to help you explain the sentences. Try to
     have a brief discussion about the topic of each of these
     sentences.

1. (Student B) , do you go to the dentist every year?
    After Student B's clarification question:
    (Student C) , could you help me explain?

2. Last night I went to a restaurant with my friends, but I
    didn't have enough money to pay for my dinner. I was
    terribly embarrassed.

3. Which would be the worst way to die: to fall out of an airplane,
    to fall off a ship, or to get lost in the desert?

4. I'm very good with animals. In fact, I was able to teach my
    dog a lot of tricks.

5. When was the last time you were a passenger on a plane,
    train, or bus?

Unit 22 continues on the next page.

Part 2

A
A
A
A
A
A
A

   (1) Student B will read some sentences to Student C.

   (2) Student C will ask Student B clarification questions.

   (3) Student B will ask you to help clarify for Student C. Help Student B explain. Try to have a brief discussion about the topic of each sentence.

Part 3

   (1) Student C will read some sentences to you.

   (2) You ask Student C the five clarification questions below.

   (3) Student C will ask Student B to help clarify the sentences for you.

1. (Student C) , what do you mean by the word "crime"?

2. I'm afraid I didn't understand what you said.

3. I don't understand the word "pre-teen."

4. What are "clubs"?

5. Can you give me some examples of "study habits"?

Helping the Discussion
Leader Explain, II

Format: Triads – Student B, page 114; Student C, page 173
Topic: Part 1. Fathers Who Live Longer
      Part 2. Smoking and Aging
      Part 3. Tasting Foods

Before Part 1 of the discussion
  (1) *Silently* read your article about fathers who live longer in Part 1.
  (2) Write answers to your *Factual Questions* and write two more questions.
  (3) Write two more *Reaction Questions* in Part 4.

Part 1
  (1) Read this article to your partners.
  (2) Don't answer your partners' clarification questions.
  (3) Ask a partner to help you explain.
  (4) Try to use the **"Help the Leader" Expressions.**
  (5) Ask your *Factual Questions.*

"Help the Leader"
Expressions

Could you help me explain that?
Do you know what I mean?

Unit 23 continues on the next page.

A
A
A
A
A
A

Fathers Who Live Longer

Researchers have found that fathers who help with child care tend to live longer than fathers who don't. In this study, researchers analyzed humans and nine species of primates (monkeys and apes) to see how males and females shared parenting duties. They found that among primates in which parents equally shared the care of their children, the life-spans of the males and females were almost the same. But, in the species in which the males took almost no interest in child-raising, the females outlived the males by many years. **Understand?**

For instance, in chimpanzees, where the adult males do almost nothing for the children, researchers found that there are about three times more adult females than adult males. However, among mountain gorillas, where the fathers protect and play with their young, adult males and females live almost the same number of years. For humans, the researchers studied 200 years of families in Sweden. They found that women tended to live five percent to eight percent longer than men. **Could you understand?**

Finally, some South American monkeys are especially interesting. The adult males always carry the babies shortly after birth except when the mother is feeding them. These adult males actually live longer than the females. **Got it?**

Factual Questions about the article

Ask these questions about the article.

1. In this study, who did the researchers analyze?

   _____

2. _____

   _____

3. _____

4. What did the article say about the South American monkey?

   _____

Parts 2 & 3

(1) Listen to your partners read their articles.

(2) For practice, ask **clarification questions**, *even if you understand clearly*.

Part 4

Reaction Questions about your partners' opinions and experiences

Child-raising Fathers

1. About this article, were you surprised to learn about the results? What do you think caused the fathers to live longer?

2. **To men**: In the future, if you have children, do you plan to be active in child caring?

   To women: In the future, if you have children, will you expect your husband to be active in child caring?

3. _____

4. _____

Discussion

A
A
A
A
A
A

Format: Triads – Student B, page 117; Student C, page 176
Topic: Gambling

Before Part 1 of the discussion

(1) *Silently* read your part of the article about gambling in Part 1.
(2) Write answers to your *Factual Questions* and write two more questions.

Part 1

(1) Read this first part of the article to your partners.
(2) Then ask them your *Factual Questions.*

Gambling (A)

There is an important expression that you need to understand before we can discuss this article. Do you understand the expression "compulsive gambler"? The word "compulsive" means that you feel a strong need to do something; in other words, you *cannot* stop yourself from doing something. It's like an addiction. For example, some people are compulsive shoppers; this means they go shopping whenever possible, even if they don't need anything. There are also compulsive chocolate-eaters, compulsive TV-watchers and compulsive gamblers.

Compulsive gamblers feel great energy and excitement when they gamble. They forget about their problems, pain, and boredom. They have fantasies about how wonderful their life will be after they win a lot of money. Even after they lose, their excitement continues and even increases, because they feel that, if they continue gambling, surely they will win soon.

Unit 24 continues on the next page.

Discussion

Factual Questions about the article

Ask these questions about the article.

A
A
A
A
A
A

1. _____

2. What do compulsive shoppers do?

   _____

   _____

3. What are some other types of compulsive habits?

   _____

   _____

4. _____

Parts 2 & 3

(1) Listen to Students B & C tell about the second and third parts of the article.

(2) Interrupt and ask clarification questions when you don't understand.

(3) Answer their *Factual Questions.*

Part 4

Reaction Questions about your partners' opinions and experiences. Ask the questions below and some follow-up questions. Answer your partners' questions with details.

Lady Luck and You

1. Have you ever gambled?
4. What do you do when you feel bored?

(Think of two more *Reaction Questions* about gambling.)

Expressing Opinions, I

Format: Pairs – Student B, page 120
Topic: Information from a Survey

Part 1: Survey
    (1) Ask five or more people these questions.
    (2) Mark their choices on the chart.

Question	Number	Question	Number
1. What is the best age for women to get married?		**6 Where is the best place to have a vacation?**	
a. 20 to 23 years old		a. at a beach resort	
b. 24 to 26 years old		b. at a mountain resort	
c. 27 years or older		c. in a famous city	
2. What do you think about watching TV?		**7. Do you feel uncomfortable around foreigners?**	
a. a waste of time		a. Yes	
b. a good use of time		b. No	
3. Do you have a serious problem at this time?		**8. What kind of movie do you prefer?**	
		a. comedy	
a. yes		b. mystery	
b. no		c. adventure	
4. Which is the better season?		**9. Do you drink coffee every day?**	
a. summer			
b. winter		a. yes	
5. What is your blood type?		b. no	
a. A		**10. What is the best sport to watch?**	
b. B		a. tennis	
c. AB		b. soccer	
d. O		c. basketball	
e. I don't know.		d. baseball	

A
A
A
A
A
A
A

Before Part 2 of the discussion

Silently read the sentences in Part 3 and choose an answer.

Part 2

(1) Listen to your partner give some opinions.

(2) Referring to your survey, agree or disagree with your partner using the expressions below.

(3) Discuss your own opinions.

Expressions for Agreeing

That's a good point. I found that most people . . .
I agree. I learned that most people . . .
You've got it right. Most people in my survey . . .

Expressions for Disagreeing

I'm afraid I disagree. I found that most people . . .
Are you sure? Actually, I learned that most people . . .
It's interesting. I found something different. Most . .

Part 3

(1) Read these sentences to your partner.

(2) Discuss your own opinions.

1. In my opinion, most people enjoy _____ during their free time.
   a. watching TV
   b. playing sports or exercising
   c. reading books or magazines

2. I feel sure most people think that _____ is the best place to study.
   a. the library
   b. their bedroom
   c. a lounge

Unit 25 continues on the next page.

3. Don't you think most people ____ ?
   a. want to live in their hometown in the future
   b. want to live someplace other than their hometown
4. I feel most people think that the perfect number of children to have would be ____.
   a. none
   b. 1
   c. 2
   d. more than 2
5. I'd bet that most people ____ .
   a. have smoked a cigarette at least once.
   b. have never smoked a cigarette
6. I believe that most people ____ feel stress in this school.
   a. often
   b. sometimes
   c. rarely
7. I think most people ____ to get exercise every day.
   a. try
   b. don't try
8. I feel sure most people think that ____.
   a. married life is better than single life
   b. single life is better than married life
9. During their high school days, I feel sure that most people enjoyed ____ the most.
   a. math
   b. science
   c. languages
   d. history
10. I imagine most people ____ around strangers.
    a. feel shy
    b. don't feel shy

Expressing Opinions, II

A
A
A
A
A
A

Format: Small Groups – B, page 123; C, page 179; D, page 182

Topics: Part 1. The Rights of Mothers and Fathers
Part 2. Death Caused by Cigarettes
Part 3. De-barking Dogs
Part 4. 63-year-old Woman Has a Baby

Agreeing

That's a good point.

I totally agree with _____.

That's right.

Disagreeing

I'm afraid I disagree.

That's a good point, but . . .

Actually, I think . . .

Before Part 1 of the discussion

Silently read this article about the rights of mothers and fathers in Part 1.

Part 1

(1) Read your article to your partners.
(2) Then ask the *Factual* and *Reaction Questions.*

Unit 26 continues on the next page.

The Rights of Mothers and Fathers

Three years ago, Gina entered Harvard University, in Boston, with a full scholarship. She planned to graduate from Harvard, go to law school, and become a lawyer. Unfortunately, in her second year she had to return to her hometown in California when she found out she had gotten pregnant during the previous summer. The father of her baby is her ex-boyfriend, Tommy, who lives in California.

Now her baby is ten months old, and Gina wants to return with her baby to Harvard to continue her studies. But Tommy, the father, doesn't want Gina to take the baby. He says the baby should stay with him in California because he could take care of the baby better than Gina could. Tommy has a job as a waiter and makes about $800 month. He says his parents (the baby's grandparents) could take care of the baby while he's working. At the same time, he says Gina would be too busy with her studies at Harvard to be a good mother. Because she has no relatives in Boston, the baby would have to spend a lot of time in daycare while Gina is in classes or studying.

Gina disagrees with Tommy. She says that, as the baby's mother, she could take better care of the baby than anyone else and that a baby needs its mother. She is confident that she could study and take care of the baby. Also, she says that the baby will have a better future if Gina can graduate from a famous university like Harvard and become a lawyer.

Factual Questions about the article

Ask these questions about the article.

1. Why does the father, Tommy, think that the baby should stay with him?
2. Why does the mother, Gina, think the baby should stay with her?

Reaction Questions about your partners' opinions. Ask these questions about the article. Agree or disagree with your partners. Express your own opinions as well.

Parenting

1. Who do you think could better take care of this baby?
2. What do you think this couple should do?

Parts 2, 3, & 4

(1) Listen to your partners read their articles.
(2) Answer and discuss their questions.

Referring to a Source

Format: Triads – Student B, page 126; Student C, page 185
Topic: Bullying

Referring to a Source

I read that _____.
I heard that _____.
According to an article I read, _____.
According to the newspaper, _____.

Before Part 1 of the discussion
(1) *Silently* read the information from the article about bullying.
(2) **Do** not **read this article to your partners.**

Bullying (A)

This article about bullying in school tells about some things that bullies do to other kids, and it explains why some kids are victims of bullying.

There are many things that bullies do to hurt other kids. Often bullies hit their victim. Also, when their victim is walking past the bully, the bully will try to trip them. It is common for bullies to call other kids names, for example, "You big fat pig," or give a cruel nickname to someone, for example, "witch." They pull other kids' hair and take away their lunch money. It is also common for bullies to ostracize someone; this means that they don't let the victim join their group or they tell their friends not to talk to the victim. This is called "the silent treatment." Some bullies do other strange things like force their victims to wear a dog

This article is continued on the next page.

Referring to a Source

A
A
A
A
A
A

collar, crawl on their knees, or eat insects. It was reported that one young bully pushed hot pins under the victim's fingernails.

Why do some kids become the victims of bullying? Often a bully chooses someone who is different from the other kids. This could be a child with a big nose, freckles, or red hair. Sometimes the child has an unusual accent. It is common for victims to be small and physically weak; however, a very tall kid can also become a victim. Some kids become victims because they're smart and others because they're not smart. For example, at one school, a girl became a victim because she answered a lot of questions in class, and a boy was bullied because he had an unusual hair-style. Many victims of bullying are shy. **Source: *Chicago Tribune***

Part 1

(1) Don't read this article to your partners.
(2) Instead, ask the following questions.
(3) After your partners answer, tell them what you have learned from the article. Don't read it to them.
(4) Try to use the expressions for **"Referring to a Source."**

Questions for your partners

1. What do you think are some things bullies do to their victims? In other words, what do bullies do to hurt other kids?
2. Why do you think some kids are victims of bullying? In other words, why do bullies choose to hurt some kids?

A
A
A
A
A
A

Parts 2 & 3

Answer your partners' questions by giving your opinion. You don't have to refer to a source.

Part 4

Discussion about your partners' opinions and experiences with bullying. Ask your partners these questions and answer their questions.

1. When you were younger, was bullying a problem in your schools?
4. If you had a younger sibling who was being bullied, what would you do?

A
A
A
A
A
A

Summary Discussion

Format: Triads – Student B, page 129; Student C, page 187
Topics: Part 1. Best Friends
           Part 2. The Effects of Watching TV
           Part 3. Spanking

Before Part 1 of the discussion
  (1) Review the Discussion Strategies with your partner(s).
  (2) First, fill in the blanks in the Summary box below by
       asking each other for examples.
  (3) Then go back to the unit where the strategy is introduced to
       review other phrases and expressions.
  (4) Then *silently* read your article in Part 1.

⎯ Discussion Strategies Summary ⎯

Rejoinders (Unit 1)	*I see.*
Follow-up Questions (Unit 1)	_____
Clarification Expressions (Unit 2)	_____
Comprehension Checks (Unit 3)	*Do you understand?*
Answering with Details (Unit 5)	_____
Interrupting (Unit 12)	_____
Words That Describe (Unit 13)	*It's a type/kind/sort of*
Telling What You've Heard (Unit 15)	_____
Volunteering an Answer (Unit 16)	_____
Summary Clarification	
Questions (Unit 19)	*You said ____ , right?*
Telling Others' Opinions (Unit 20)	_____
Helping the Leader (Unit 22)	_____
Expressing Opinions (Unit 25)	*That's a good point, but*
	I'm afraid I disagree.
Referring to a Source (Unit 27)	_____

GUYS... WE'RE 10 YEARS OLD NOW,
I THINK IT'S TIME FOR A
COMMITMENT

Summary Discussion

Part 1

> (1) Read this article to your partners.
> (2) Then discuss it, using the strategies above.

A
A
A
A
A
A

Best Friends

This article tells about some things that researchers found out about children's best friends. First of all, they found out that having only one best friend is common among adults, but it isn't common among pre-school children. Pre-school children will often say they have two or three best friends. For these pre-school children, their best friends are simply the children they play with most. On the other hand, when children are about ten years old, they choose their best friends according to personality.

Researchers also found that the number of friends for boys and girls is different. It's common for girls of school age to have one best friend, but boys usually have several good friends. Even at two years old, boys have more friends than girls do. Girls like to talk about their thoughts and feelings with a friend, so often they spend more time in pairs. Boys, on the other hand, spend more time in big groups.

Parts 2 and 3

> (1) Listen to Students B and C read their articles.
> (2) Then discuss their articles with them, using discussion strategies.

Part 4

Discuss your discussion

> (1) Did you use a lot of the strategies?
> (2) Which ones did you use?
> Which ones didn't you use? Why not?

┌ Rejoinders ┐	┌ Follow-up Questions ┐
I see.	*(Questions about an answer)*
Oh, yeah?	**A: What did you do last night?**
Really?	**B: I watched a movie on TV.**
That's great!	**A:** *(Rejoinder and Follow-up)* **I see.**
That's too bad.	**What movie did you watch?**

Format: Triads – Student A, page 1; Student C, page 133

Before the discussion
   (1) *Silently* complete the questions below.
   (2) Write two more questions about any topic.

Discussion Directions
   (1) Ask *both* of your partners your discussion questions.
   (2) After they answer, ask **follow-up questions** and use **rejoinders**.
   (3) Take turns. Student A begins with question #1. You ask #2, then Student C asks #3, and you continue.
   (4) Answer your partners' questions *with details*.

Discussion Questions
  2. What time do you prefer to _____?

  5. Do you have any _____?

  8. Where have you _____ recently?

11. Were you a good student when you were young?

14. Which member of your family _____?

17. Are you _____?

20. _____?

23. _____?

   Note: Follow-up questions frequently use WH-questions.

What movie?	Where did you see it?
Who was in it?	Why did you choose that one?
What did you think of it?	How long was it?
How often do you go to the movies?	

Student B • Unit 2 ᐧ◠ᐤ

—— Clarification Expressions ——

Pardon?
Excuse me. } {
What/Who/Where did you say _____ is?
Did you say _____?
You said _____, right?
You did what?
I'm afraid I didn't understand that.

Format: Pairs – Student A, page 2

Before Part 1 of the discussion
   Without talking to your partner, fill in the blanks in Part 2.

Part 1
   (1) Listen to your partner. Using **clarification expressions**, ask
       for clarification *after each sentence*, even if you understand clearly.
   (2) After your partner answers, ask *follow-up questions* (see Unit 1)
       in order to have a brief discussion about the topic in each sentence.

1. *After sentence 1, ask:* Did you say that you're going to buy _____?
2. Pardon? *Who* would you like to meet?
3 -10. (Ask for **clarification** after each sentence.)

Part 2 Note: When there are choices in parentheses, choose one. Example, (yes/no/maybe)
   (1) Read your sentences to your partner and respond to their
       clarification expressions.
   (2) Try to have a brief discussion about the topic in each sentence.

1. In the future, I want to work in a _____.
2. I think computers are _____.
3. This coming weekend, I think you should _____.
4. If I could change one physical thing about myself, I'd change _____.
5. My favorite _____ is _____.
6. I have a secret to tell you. I heard that _____.
7. If I were an author, I would write about _____.
8. I would rather win (an Olympic gold medal/an Academy Award/
   a Nobel Prize) than win (an Olympic gold medal/an Academy
   Award/a Nobel Prize).
9. (My friend /I) got angry because _____.
10. I need some advice about _____. Could you advise me?

Clarification Expressions

Clarification Questions, I
Comprehension Checks

(Do you) understand _____?
OK?   (Have you) got it?

Focus: Sentence-by-sentence clarifications with questions provided
Format: Pairs – Student A, page 3
Topics: Part 1. Flight Attendant Hero
Part 2. Lost in a Jungle

Before Part 1 of the discussion
(1) *Silently* read your article in Part 2.
(2) Write answers to the *Factual Questions* about the article.

Part 1
(1) Listen to your partner read a news article.
(2) *After each sentence*, your partner will ask a **comprehension
check**. In response, ask one of the **clarification questions**
below. There are nine sentences.
(3) Then answer the *Factual Questions* and *Reaction Questions*.

Clarification Questions

Flight Attendant Hero

1. Could you tell me what a "flight attendant" is?
2. Which airline?
3. Where was the plane going?
4. Could you repeat that, please?
5. Did you say it was cloudy or clear?
6. What did she tell the pilot?
7. I didn't understand that. Could you explain it?
8. Could you explain what the word "rescue" means?
9. Did you say the helicopter was taking pictures of fish?

Factual Questions about the article
Answer your partner's questions.

Reaction Questions about your opinions and experiences
Try to answer all your partner's questions and follow-up
questions *with details*.   *Unit 3 is continued on the next page.*

Part 2

(1) Read this article to your partner.

(2) *Stop after each sentence* and ask your **comprehension check**.

(3) In response, your partner will ask a **clarification question**.

(4) When you have finished all the sentences, ask your partner the *Factual Questions* and *Reaction Questions*.

B
B
B
B
B
B

Lost in a Jungle

1. This story took place in the Amazon rain forest in South America.
   Do you understand this first sentence?

2. Two sisters, one 9 and the other 13, were going on a walking trip with their uncle; they were going from their home to his farm, which was in the middle of the rain forest. The uncle's farm was about 320 kilometers from their home.
   Understand this next part?

3. The uncle suddenly died from malaria, so the sisters had to walk back to their home through the rain forest by themselves.
   OK?

4. They hadn't brought any food with them, so they had to eat wild fruit and sometimes a fish.
   Do you understand this fourth part?

5. They had only one box of matches and they found some wax or gum from a certain tree. They used it to cook and to make candles for light.
   Do you understand what I just said?

6. In this forest, there were lots of snakes, crocodiles, and jaguars (a big cat).
   OK?

7. They had a frightening experience when a jaguar saw them and ran toward them; fortunately, they were able to climb a tree to escape.
   Understand this seventh part?

8. After 31 days in the forest someone saw them and saved them, but one sister was very sick because she drank dirty water from a river.
   Got it?

9. When they were found, the girls also had big red mosquito bites all over their bodies. Now, however, they're all right.
   Do you understand this last part?

Unit 3 is continued on the next page.

Clarification Questions, I

Factual Questions about the article

Ask your partner the following questions.

1. Where did this story take place?

_____

2. Why were these girls in the rain forest alone?

_____

3. What were some dangerous things in this forest?

_____

4. How many days were they alone in this forest?

_____

5. What kinds of food did they eat?

_____

6. In the end, did the sisters have any health problems?

_____

Reaction Questions about your partner's opinions and experiences. Ask these questions and ask *follow-up questions.*

1. Have you ever gotten lost, when you were either walking or driving somewhere?
2. Do you ever spend time hiking or camping in a forest?
3. What's the most dangerous thing that happened to you as a child?
4. Tell me about a scary or surprising experience you had with a sibling (your brother or sister) or with a friend.
5. What underdeveloped part of the world would you like to visit?

(Think of some *Reaction Questions* about this topic.)

6. _____

7. _____

B
B
B
B
B
B

Clarification Questions, II

Focus: Sentence-by-sentence clarifications, questions *not* provided
Format: Pairs – Student A, page 6
Topics: Part 1. Giant Baby
Part 2. Music, Reading, and Math

Before Part 1 of the duscussion

(1) *Silently* read your article in Part 2.
(2) Write answers to the *Factual Questions* about the article.

Part 1

(1) Listen to your partner read a news article.
(2) *After each sentence*, your partner will ask a **comprehension check**. In response, ask a **clarification question**.
Samples are given below. *Even if you understand clearly,* ask a clarification question for practice.

B
B
B
B
B
B

⎯ Sample Clarification Questions ⎯

Did you say _____?
Could explain what a _____ is?
Why did _____?
How many _____?
Who/What/Where/When/Why did you say _____?
I'm afraid I didn't understand that. Could you repeat it?

Factual Questions about the article

Answer your partner's questions.

Reaction Questions about your opinions and experiences

Try to answer the questions *with details*.

Unit 4 is continued on the next page.

Clarification Questions, II

Part 2

   (1) Read this article to your partner.

   (2) *Stop after each sentence* and ask your comprehension check.

   (3) In response, your partner will ask a **clarification question**.

   (4) When you have finished all the sentences, ask your partner the *Factual Questions* and *Reaction Questions*.

Music, Reading, and Math

1. Researchers found that students can improve their reading and math scores by studying music.
   Do you understand this first sentence?

2. They found that there is a connection between math and music, so they said that parents should add music to their children's education.
   Understand?

3. In this research, they gave reading and math tests to 96 children between the ages of 4 and 6.
   Got it?

4. After that, the children were divided into 2 groups: one group got Music lessons every day and the other group didn't.
   OK?

5. The next year, they gave all the students the same reading and math tests again and compared their scores from the year before.
   Did you understand what I just said?

6. The researchers found that the students who had received the lessons in music improved a lot on the math and reading tests.
   Got it?

7. Some students who were below-average readers became average readers after getting the extra music lessons.
   Understand?

8. The researchers said they were not surprised at the results because many people who are good in music are also good in math. For example, Albert Einstein, who was a math genius, loved to play the violin.
   Did you understand that?

B
B
B
B
B
B

Unit 4 is continued on the next page.

Factual Questions about the article
Ask your partner the following questions.

1. What skills improved after studying music?

   _____

2. How many children were in the study? (a) 76 (b) 96 (c) 106
   (d) 126

   _____

3. Were the children teenagers?

   _____

4. What types of lessons did half of the children get?

   _____

5. When did they give the children reading and math tests?

   _____

6. Which students' scores improved a lot?

   _____

7. Were the researchers surprised?

   _____

8. What instrument did Albert Einstein love to play?

   _____

Reaction Questions about your partner's opinions and experiences. Ask these questions and ask follow-up questions.

Music, Reading, and Math

1. Were you surprised to hear about the results of this research?
2. Did your parents encourage you to study music when you were a child?
3. Did you like school when you were a child?
4. Are you good in math?
5. What musical instrument would you like to be able to play very well?
6. During what part of the day do you like to listen to music?
7. What types of things did you like to read when you were a child?
8. Nowadays, how many hours a day do you spend reading?

More Clarification Questions

Answering with Details

Format: Triads – Student A, page 9; Student C, page 134

Before the discussion
(1) *Silently* read and answer the questions below for yourself, but *do not write the answers.*
(2) Write two more questions about any topic.

Discussion directions
(1) Ask these questions of *both* of your partners.
(2) After they answer, ask them follow-up questions.
(3) Answer their questions *with details* by using **and, but, so, because,** or **two sentences** each time you answer.

Discussion Questions

Some Personal Questions

2. What is the most challenging thing about learning English?

5. Which would you prefer to be: a) very smart b) very athletic c) very artistic?

8. Are you optimistic or pessimistic about your future? In other words, do you have a positive or negative feeling about your future?

11. Are you a competitive-type person?

14. Is your best friend a male or a female?

17. What is one thing you would like to change about yourself or your life?

20. _____?

23. _____?

Discussion

Discussion

Format: Triads – Student A, page 11; Student C, page 135
Topic: Your High School Days

Before the discussion

(1) *Silently* read the questions below, but *do not write* the answers.
(2) Write two more questions about the topic.

Discussion directions

(1) Ask these questions of *both* of your partners.
(2) After they answer, ask them **follow-up questions**, and use **rejoinders** (e.g., "I see," "That's too bad," or "That's great!").
    [Note: "e.g." is an academic abbreviation meaning "for example."]
(3) Also, answer your partners' questions *with details*.

Discussion Questions

Your High School Days

2. Where was your high school (e.g., in the countryside or in the middle of a city)?
5. What type of clothes did you wear (e.g., did you wear a uniform)?
8. In general, did you spend your free time with other high school kids, or did you spend time alone?
11. What did you usually do after school?
14. Did you ever have a part-time job in those days?
17. In general, what kind of relationship did you have with your teachers (good, bad, or average)?
20. How were your grades in high school (good, average, or low)?
23. How many people were in your class?
26. Did you take any special trips with your classmates?
29. What subjects were you good at?
32. How many boyfriends (if you're a girl) or girlfriends (if you're a boy) did you have?
35. What kind of hair style did you have then?
38. _____
41. _____

Student B • Unit 7 ∽

Paragraph Clarifications, I

Focus: Paragraph-by-paragraph clarifications, with clarification questions provided

Format: Triads – Student A, page 12; Student C, page 137

Topic: Animals in Movies

Before Part 1 of the discussion

(1) *Silently* read your part (B) of the article about animals in movies in Part 1.

(2) Write the answers to the *Factual Questions* in Part 4.

Part 1

(1) Listen to Student A tell the first part of the story.

(2) *After each paragraph*, ask the appropriate **clarification question** below.

PARAGRAPH 1: Are you talking about movies?

PARAGRAPH 2: Can you tell me again what the AHS does?

PARAGRAPH 3: Why did the cowboy jump off a cliff?

Part 2:

(1) Read this second part of the story (B) to your partners.

(2) *Stop after each paragraph* to ask your **comprehension check.**

(3) Then answer your partners' **clarification questions.**

Animals in Movies (B)

4. Let's continue with this story about animals in movies. Have you seen a movie in which a group of soldiers or cowboys is riding horses into a battle? Sometimes it looks as though the horses are shot and fall down. Actually, these horses are specially trained to fall down. They're never hurt when they do this.

   Do you understand the fourth paragraph?

5. Moviemakers also use another technique called "animal-tronics" technology. In this, they make electronic animals that look like real animals.

   Got it?

The article is continued on the next page.

---

6. There's a movie in which elephants jump out of an airplane with parachutes. Actually, these were all electronic elephants that the audience saw floating down from the sky. They were *not* real elephants.
   Understand paragraph 6?

Part 3
(1) Listen to Student C tell the third part of the story.
(2) *After each paragraph*, ask the **appropriate clarification question** below.

PARAGRAPH 7:   What does movie set mean?
PARAGRAPH 8:   What did you say that the AHS did for the fish?
PARAGRAPH 9:   I don't understand "cockroaches."

Part 4

Factual Questions about the story
   Ask your partners the following questions.

5. In movies with soldiers or cowboys, what sometimes happens to horses?

_____

6. Are these horses hurt when they fall down? Why (not)?

_____

7. What are "animal-tronics"?

_____

8. In the movie with the elephants, what did the elephants do?

_____

Reaction Questions about your partners' opinions and experiences. Ask these questions and ask follow-up questions.

You, Animals, and the Movies

2. Would you like to work with animals, for example, taking care of them or training them?
5. How much does a ticket to a movie cost in your country?
8. What movie have you seen recently?
11. (Think of some questions about movies and animals.)

Paragraph Clarifications, I   • **79**

Student B • Unit 8 ⟶

Paragraph Clarifications, II

Focus: Paragraph-by-paragraph clarifications, clarification
questions *not* provided
Format: Triads – Student A, page 14; Student C, page 139
Topic: Sleep

Before Part 1 of the discussion
(1) *Silently* read your part (B) of the article about sleep in Part 2.
(2) Write the answers to the *Factual Questions* about the article.

Part 1
(1) Listen to your partner (A) read the first part of the article.
(2) When they ask if you understand, ask **your own
clarification questions,** *even if you understand clearly.*

Part 2
(1) Read this first part of the story to your partners.
(2) *Stop after each paragraph* to ask your **comprehension check.**
(3) Answer your partners' **clarification questions.**
(4) Then ask your partners your *Factual Questions.*

Sleep (B)

4. About 100 million Americans are sleep-deprived. This means
they don't get enough sleep. Most people get only 7 hours of
sleep each night, but they *need* 8 to 8 1/2 hours. If you're sleepy
during the day, it means you're not sleeping enough at night.
   Do you understand that paragraph?

5. Here is some advice about good sleeping habits. First, you
should try to sleep without interruptions. This means you should
sleep for 8 hours straight. You should *not* sleep for 5 hours, get
up and do something, and then go back to bed and sleep for 3
more hours.
   OK?

The article is continued on the next page.

Paragraph Clarifications, II

6. Second, you should go to sleep at the same time every night and get up at the same time each morning. You should *not* need an alarm clock to wake you up. Many people have trouble going to sleep on Sunday nights because they sleep late Saturday and Sunday mornings. **Got it?**

Factual Questions about the article

1. How many million Americans are sleep-deprived: a) 10 b) 50 c) 100 d) 150? _____

2. Do most people get 8 hours of sleep every night? _____

3. How many hours do most people need?
_____

4. Is it good to sleep for 5 hours, get up and do something, and then sleep 3 more hours? _____

5. Why do some people have trouble falling asleep on Sunday nights?
_____

6. Should you need an alarm clock to wake you up?
_____

Part 3
(1) Listen to your partner (A) read the first part of the article.
(2) When they ask if you understand, ask your own
    clarification questions, *even if you understand clearly.*

Part 4
Reaction Questions about your partners' opinions and experiences. Ask these questions and ask follow-up questions.

Sleeping Habits
2. Usually, when you go to bed, do you fall asleep after 1 or 2 minutes or after 10 minutes?
5. Do you have trouble staying awake during your classes? How about in high school?
8. Is there a type of music that makes you feel sleepy or that you listen to before going to bed?
11. When you feel sleepy, what do you do to feel more awake?
14. (Think of two more questions about **sleep** and ask your partners.)

Paragraph Clarifications, II   • *81*

Student B • Unit 9 ⌒
Asking for More Details

Could you give me an example of _____?
What do you mean _____?
Could you explain _____?
Could you tell me why/who/what _____?
I'd like to know more about _____.

Format: Triads – Student A, page 16; Student C, page 141

Before the discussion
   (1) *Silently* read the sentences below and fill in the blanks.

Discussion Directions
   (1) Read these sentences to your partners.
   (2) Listen to your partners' sentences. **Ask them for more details**.

B
B
B
B
B
B

Discussion Starters

2. _____ makes me angry.

5. When I'm at a party, I _____

8. One thing I'd like to change about my childhood would be ___
_____

11. If I get married, I want my spouse to _____
_____

14. I wish _____
were still alive today.

17. _____ is the best time of day to _____
_____

Discussion

Format: Triads – Student A, page 17; Student C, page 142
Topic: Stress

Before Part 1 of the discussion
(1) **Silently** read your part (B) of the article about stress in Part 2.
(2) Write answers to the *Factual Questions* after the article and then write two more questions.

Part 1
(1) Listen to your partner (A) read the first part of the article.
(2) Ask clarification questions when you don't understand.
(3) Answer the *Factual Questions* your partner asks.

Part 2
(1) Read this second part of the article (B) to your partners.
(2) Answer any clarification questions they have.
(3) Ask them your *Factual Questions*.

B
B
B
B
B
B

Stress (B)

Let's continue with the second part of the article. Researchers also studied 90 married couples (of people, not monkeys). First they took blood samples from the couples. **Do you understand "blood samples"?** Then they asked the couples to find the solution to a disagreement that they had. Some couples argued and had a fight. Other couples were friendly in their discussion. **Understand?** After 24 hours, the researchers took another blood sample from the couples. The blood of the couples who had fought had changed. The blood samples showed that their bodies' ability to fight sickness had become worse. In other words, their condition was weaker after the stress of fighting. **Got it?**

This article is continued on the next page.

The friendliest monkeys were the healthiest

> Researchers also studied stress among college students
> when they were taking exams. They found that students
> who had close friends and family members had better
> health after the stress of taking exams.
> **Do you understand?**

Factual Questions about the article

1. What kind of sample did they take from the married couples?

_____

2. What did they tell the married couples to talk about?

_____

3.

_____

4.

_____

Part 3

    (1) Listen to your partner (C) read the last part of the article.
    (2) Ask clarification questions when you don't understand.
    (3) Answer the Factual Questions your partner asks.

Part 4

Reaction Questions about your partners' opinions and experiences. Ask the questions below, and ask follow-up questions. Also, answer your partners' questions with details.

Stress in Our Lives

2. When you were in elementary or high school, did you feel stress? What caused it?
5. Do you prefer to spend time with the same friends, or do you like to meet new people? Why?

(Think of two more *Reaction Questions*.)

Discussion

Discussion

Format: Triads – Student A, page 21; Student C, page 145
Topic: Your Hometown and Childhood Home

Before the discussion

(1) *Silently* read the discussion questions below, but **do not write** the answers.
(2) Write two more questions about the topic of your hometown and childhood home.

Discussion Directions

(1) Ask *both of* your partners your discussion questions.
(2) Try to use these *discussion strategies.*

Discussion Strategies

Ask **follow-up questions** and **solicit more details.**
  (e.g., "Could you give me an example?" "What do you mean_____?" or "Could you explain _____?")
Use **rejoinders**
  (e.g., "I see," "That's too bad," or "That's great!")
Answer questions **with details.**
  (e.g., answer with *and, but, so, because,* or with *two sentences.*)

B
B
B
B
B
B

Discussion Questions

Your Hometown and Childhood Home

2. What is your hometown famous for?

5. When you're older, do you want to live in your hometown?

8. What's the best season in your hometown?

11. Did you have any computers in your house?

14. Is there anything about your house that you did not like?

17. Was it generally noisy, or quiet, in your neighborhood?

20. _____

23. _____

Interrupting Someone

Excuse me. Could I ask something?
Uhh, sorry for interrupting, but . . .
Excuse me, but I have a question.

Format: Triads – Student A, page 22; Student C, page 146
Topic: Telling lies

Before Part 1 of the discussion
(1) **Silently** read your part (B) of the article on telling lies
in Part 2.
(2) Write answers to your *Factual Questions* about the article.

Part 1
(1) Listen to Student A read the first part of the article.
(2) Interrupt *while* Student A is reading and ask **some**
clarification questions *even if you understand clearly.*
(3) Try to use the **"Interrupting Someone"** expressions.

For example: I'm sorry for interrupting, but I have a question.
What kind of lies are called fibs?

Part 2:
(1) Read this second part of the article (B) to your partners.
(2) **Don't ask them if they understand,** but answer their
clarification questions when they interrupt you.
(3) When you're finished, ask them your *Factual Questions.*

Telling Lies (B)

This is the second part of the article about telling lies.
Researchers found that there are two types of lies. The
first type is the "self-centered" lie. This is a lie that we
tell to help ourselves or to make ourselves look important.

This article is continued on the next page.

We also tell self-centered lies because we're embarrassed. For example, let's say you borrowed your friend's bicycle and you accidentally broke something on it. When you return the bike to your friend, you tell your friend that part of the bike was broken before you got it. This is a self-centered lie; you told it because you were embarrassed, or because you didn't want to pay for the repairs. In general, the self-centered lie is one of the most common types people tell.

The second type of lie is most common among women. It's called the "polite" lie. We tell this lie to make another person feel good. For example, let's say you hate snow and cold weather. One day there's a snowstorm in your town. You meet your friend who loves skiing, and she says, "Isn't this snow wonderful!" You answer by saying, "Yes, it's great," even though you think it's awful. This is an example of a "polite" lie.

B
B
B
B
B
B

Factual Questions about the article

1. Why do people tell self-centered lies?

2. Are self-centered lies uncommon?

3. What type of lie is most common among women?

4. Give me an example of a polite lie.

Unit 12 is continued on the next page.

Interrupting Someone

Part 3

Listen to Student C, interrupt, and ask clarification questions.

For example: Please, I'm sorry to interrupt, but what kind of people are called "introverts"?

Part 4

Reaction Questions about your partners' opinions and experiences. Ask these questions and follow-up questions.

To Lie or Not to Lie

2. Let's say you're at a store and you buy something. It costs $8. You give the sales clerk $10. The clerk gives you back $5 in change. Would you tell the clerk about the mistake?

5. Let's say you had some homework to do, but instead of doing it, you went to a movie with a friend. The next day at school, your teacher asks you why you don't have your homework. Would you lie or tell the truth?

8. When you tell a lie, do you worry about getting caught?

11. In general, do you trust your friends to always tell you the truth, or do you think they sometimes lie to you?

Words That Describe

Expressions

It is a person/animal/place/thing that _____.
It is an event/condition/situation that _____.
It is a type/kind/sort of _____.
You can find it at/in _____.

Format: Triads – Student A, page 25; Student C, page 149

Before starting
  (1) ***Silently*** look at the words in the list below.
  (2) *Don't show or tell your words to your partners.*

Directions
  (1) Take turns. Using the expressions above, describe your words to your partners.
  (2) Don't say the word.
  (3) Your partners will try to guess the word.
  (4) If they can't guess the word, they can ask a question.

B
B
B
B
B
B

flight attendant	salary	computer
neighborhood	genius	helicopter
text message	cowboy	habit
caffeine	party	cliff

Dropping a butterknife during a meal means a male visitor is forthcoming

B
B
B
B
B
B

Discussion

Format: Triads – Student A, page 27; Student C, page 151
Topic: Superstitions

Before Part 1 of the discussion
(1) **Silently** read your part of the article (B) in Part 2 below.
(2) Write answers to the *Factual Questions* and write two more questions.

Part 1
(1) Listen to Student A read the first part of the article.
(2) *Interrupt and ask clarification questions* when you don't understand.
(3) Answer your partner's *Factual Questions*.

Part 2
(1) Read this second part of the article to your partners.
(2) Then ask them your *Factual Questions*.

B
B
B
B
B
B

Superstitions (B)

According to Russians, we will have bad luck if we whistle indoors, celebrate a birthday in advance, or return something that we borrowed at night. They also believe colors can be lucky or unlucky. For example, yellow flowers are considered sad and so unlucky. Also, red can be unlucky. Russians are suspicious of someone with red hair, because there are very few redheads in Russia. **OK so far?**

Some superstitions are connected to traditional religious beliefs. For example, there was a belief that all travelers were guarded by their own personal angel. If you started on a trip but had to return home because you forgot something, your angel would wait for you along the roadside where you turned around. So,

This article is continued on the next page.

when you returned home, it was important that you looked in the mirror, stuck out your tongue, and made an ugly face in order to scare away any evil spirits in your house and to bring your angel back to you before you started off on your trip again. **OK?**

Factual Questions about the article

1. According to Russians, when is whistling bad luck?

_____

2. How do Russians feel about people with red hair? Why do they feel this way?

_____

3.

_____

4.

_____

B
B
B
B
B
B

Part 3

(1) Listen to Student C read the last part of the article.
(2) *Interrupt and ask clarification questions* when you don't understand.
(3) Answer your partner's *Factual Questions*.

Part 4

Reaction Questions about your partners' opinions and experiences.

(1) Ask these questions and follow-up questions.
(2) Answer your partners' questions with details.

It's Your Lucky Day

2. In your country what do people think causes *bad* luck?
5. Do you do anything for good luck before taking a test or playing a game?

(Think of two more *Reaction Questions* about superstitions.)

Discussion

Telling What You've Heard

Phrases for Telling

A told me about . . . .
B said (that) . . . .
C told me (that) . . . .
B explained (that) . . . .
According to A, ...

Format: **Triads** – Student A, page 29; Student C, page 153

Topics: Part 1. Short People Live Longer
Part 2. Gossiping
Part 3. Why the French Have Fewer Heart Attacks

Before Part 1 of the discussion
(1) *Silently* read your article in Part 2.
(2) Write the answers to the *Factual Questions* about the article.

Part 1
(1) Listen to Student A tell you about the article, "Short People Live Longer." *Don't take notes.*
(2) Tell Student C about the article.
(3) Student C will answer Student A's *Factual Questions* about the article. *Don't answer or help.*

Part 2
(1) Tell only Student C about your article, "Gossiping."
(2) Do not tell Student A.
(3) Student C will tell A what they heard about the article.
(4) Ask Student A your *Factual Questions below.*

Unit 15 is continued on the next page.

Gossiping

This article is about gossiping. Do you understand what "gossip" is? In conversations, when people sometimes talk about other people's private lives, it is called gossiping. We often imagine older women telling gossip to each other; in other words, they tell personal information about other people.

Researchers analyzed girls and boys between the ages of 9 and 12 in order to learn if they gossip and what they gossip about. By the way, children between 9 and 12 are called "pre-teens." The researchers found that pre-teens spend 50% of their conversation time gossiping.

Girls often talked about boys that they were in love with. They also talked about boys that other girls loved. Boys, on the other hand, rarely talked about special girls they loved. But they did talk about girls in general.

There was some interesting information about pre-teens. Pairs of boys who were good friends gossiped less than boys who were not close friends. In other words, boys used gossip to become friends with someone new. Girls, on the other hand, used gossip mostly with their best friends. Girls spent much more time gossiping with close friends than with girls who were just acquaintances.

B
B
B
B
B
B

Factual Questions about the article

1. What word means "having conversations about other people's private lives?"

_____

2. How old are "pre-teens?"

_____

Continued on the next page.

Telling What You've Heard

3. How much of pre-teens' conversations was gossip? (a) 25%
   (b) 50% (c) 75%

4. What did girls often gossip about?

_____

5. Did boys talk about girls whom they were in love with?

_____

6. Who did boys most often gossip with?

_____

Part 3

(1) Leave your group and sit in a different part of the room.
    Do not listen to Student C's article.
(2) After Student C tells Student A about the article, come
    back to the group. Student A will explain the article to you.
(3) Answer Student C's *Factual Questions* about the article.

B
B
B
B
B
B

Part 4

**Reaction Questions about your partners' opinions and
experiences.** Discuss the article, "Gossiping."

Your Feelings about Gossip

6. Do people in your country gossip?
7. When you were a pre-teen, did you talk about boys or girls
   that you loved?
8. In general, when you were in junior high and high school,
   what types of things did you talk about with your friends?
9. When you were a pre-teen, did you have a few close friends
   or many friends who were not so close?
10. Nowadays, what types of things do you talk about with your
    friends?

Volunteering an Answer

Phrases for Volunteering

> I think (that) . . . .
> In my opinion, ...
> I'd like to say (that) . . . .
> May I say (that) . . . .
> Can I answer that?
> Can I respond to that?

Format: Small Groups – Student A, page 32; C, D, E 156-158

Directions for Asking

(1) Ask your questions below in any order.

(2) ***Do not ask anyone directly.*** (In other words, don't look at anyone or say anyone's name.)

(3) Your partners will volunteer to answer.

Directions for Volunteering

(1) ***Volunteer to answer*** your partners' questions ***with details.*** (Answer with **and, but, so, because,** or ***two sentences***.)

(2) Try to answer first sometimes, and sometimes wait for your partners to volunteer.

(3) Ask follow-up questions, too.

Questions for volunteers to answer

- Do you have any older brothers or sisters?

- Where and when do you remember staying in a hotel?

- Do you believe in ghosts?

- Which do you prefer, texting, talking on a cell phone, or sending emails?

- If you had to change your name, what name would you want?

Discussion

Format: **Triads** – Student A, page 33; Student C, page 159
Topic: Divorce

Part 1

Pre-discussion
   (1) Before starting this discussion about divorce in Europe, ask your partners these questions.
   (2) Answer their questions.

2. In Europe, where do you think the divorce rate is higher, in northern countries like Sweden or in southern countries like Italy?
5. Among European men, what do you think is the average age for marriage: (a) 22, (a) 24, (a) 26, (a) 28?

Part 2

Discussion Directions
   (1) Listen to Student A read the first part of the article.
   (2) Read your part of the article to your partners.
   (3) Listen to Student C read the third part of the article.

B
B
B
B
B
B

DIVORCE (B)

There is another interesting change in European marriage patterns. It is that many Europeans are getting married at a later age. The average age for women to get married for the first time is 25; for men, it's 28.

The increased divorce rate and the later age of marriage are having some interesting effects. In general, there are fewer children born nowadays, but there are more children born outside of marriage. In other words, nowadays, more children

The article is continued on the next page.

Discussion

HEY! WHERE'S THE CANDLES?.. WE USED TO HAVE CANDLES EVERY NIGHT ... are you listening to me?

Many Young People feel it is important to have a Romantic Relationship...... They expect to have a perfect marriage

are born to women who are not married. In Iceland almost 60% of children are born outside of marriage. The reason for this might be that in Iceland, a Scandinavian country, women are more independent financially, so they can raise children by themselves.

In Italy, a Catholic country, only 7% of children are born outside of marriage. However, there are some interesting effects concerning birth rates in Italy. Because many couples are getting married at a later age, Italy's birth rate has dropped sharply. About 20 years ago, Italy had the highest birth rate in Europe; today, it has the lowest.

Part 3

Factual Questions about the article

Read the questions in Part 1 to your partners again and try to answer their questions.

Part 4

Reaction Questions about your partners' opinions and experiences.

Your Feelings about Marriage and Divorce

2. Is it easy for women in your country to make enough money to survive if they get divorced?
5. If you wanted a divorce, do you think your parents would pressure you to stay married?
8. What would be your reasons for getting a divorce if you had no children? What would they be if you had children?

B
B
B
B
B
B

Student B • Unit 18
Clarifying by Summarizing, I

Focus: Summarizing (clarifications are provided)
Format: Pairs – Student A, page 36
Topics: Part 1. Getting Fat Part 2. Bugs in Manila
              Wrong Stadium   Naked in the Laundromat

Before Part 1 of the discussion
(1) *Silently* read your two articles in Part 2.
(2) Write answers to the *Factual Questions* about the articles.

Part 1
(1) Listen to your partner read two articles.
(2) *After each article*, ask these **summary clarification questions**.
(3) Then answer your partner's *Factual Questions* and *Reaction Questions*.

Summary Clarification Questions

About the first article
1. You said this story happened in Africa and that the men in a certain tribe there think fat women are beautiful, right?
2. So, if a woman sees a fat man, she thinks he is rich?
3. You mean the man lay in bed for 12 weeks because he drank 19 liters of milk a day and got sick?

About the second article
1. Did you say there was a football game between two teams and an airplane was going to fly into the stadium?
2. In other words, the reason the pilot got lost was probably that he wasn't experienced, right?
3. I'm not sure I understand. You said some people watching the football game thought they saw terrorists. Why did they think they were terrorists?

Factual Questions about the articles
Answer your partner's questions.

Reaction Questions about your opinions and experiences
Try to answer your partner's questions *with details*.

Part 2

(1) Read these two articles to your partner.
(2) *After each article,* answer your partner's **summary clarification questions**.
(3) Then ask the *Factual Questions* and *Reaction Questions*.

Bugs in Manila

I also have two stories to tell you. The first story is about a problem in the Philippines. In the capital city, Manila, they have a lot of insects, for example flies and cockroaches, and they're having problems getting rid of them. **Did you understand the first part?** In order to stop the insects, the government is paying people to kill them. So if someone brings 10 flies to the police station, they will get 4 cents. If they bring in 10 cockroaches, the government will pay them 6 cents. **Did you get the second part?** Because people can make money killing insects, some people have secretly started to raise cockroaches. In other words, now there are roach farms. **Understand?**

B
B
B
B
B
B

Naked in the Laundromat

The second story happened in Canada. One day at about 4 a.m. a man went to a laundromat to wash the clothes that he was wearing. Because it was so early in the morning, nobody else was in the laundromat. **Understand the first part?** So the man took off all his clothes and put them in the washing machine. After he put all his clothes in the washer, he realized that it was very cold because he was naked. In other words, he had no clothes on. So, in order to get warm, he turned on one of the

This news story continues on the next page.

clothes dryers and got inside of it. **Did you get the second part?** While he was in the dryer, he fell asleep. A little while later, another customer came into the laundromat to do her laundry. Suddenly she noticed the naked man in the drier. She thought he was dead. So she called the police and an ambulance. When they arrived they woke the naked man and everyone was surprised. **Understand?**

Factual Questions about the articles

1. About the first article, what did the government pay people to do? Why? _____

_____

2. Which could you get more money for: 10 flies or 10 cockroaches?

_____

3. What are roach farms?

_____

4. About the second story, why was the man the only person in the laundromat? _____

_____

5. Why was the man naked?

_____

6. What happened after the customer came into the laundromat?

_____

_____

Reaction Questions about your partner's opinions and experiences. Ask these questions and ask follow-up questions.

Two Articles

1. Do people in your country have problems with things like insects, mice, or snakes?
2. Do insects bother you a lot? Are you interested in them?
3. How often do you do laundry? What do you usually do while you wait to wash and dry your laundry?
4. Tell me about a time you stayed up until 4 a.m.
5. Tell me about a time the police talked to you.

Clarifying by Summarizing, I

Clarifying by Summarizing, II

Focus: Summarizing (clarifications are not provided)
Format: Triads – Student A, page 40; Student C, page 162
Topic: Catching Colds

Before Part 1 of the discussion

(1) *Silently* read this second part of the article (B) in Part 2.
(2) Write answers to the *Factual Questions* in Part 4.

Part 1

(1) Listen to Student A read the first part of the article on colds.
(2) Ask **summary clarification questions** when asked if
   you understand, *even if you do understand clearly.*
(3) Use the following expressions.

Summary Clarification Questions

Did you say _____?   **You mean _____?**

You said _____, right?   **In other words, _____, right?**

I think you said _____, right?

I'm not sure I understand. Did you say _____?

B
B
B
B
B
B

Part 2

(1) Read this middle part of the article to your partners.
(2) Answer their **summary clarification questions**.

Catching Colds (B)

How do people catch colds? We almost always catch a cold
because we touched something dirty with our hands and then
touched our nose, mouth, or eyes. Here's what usually happens.
A person has a cold. This person blows his nose and gets
cold germs on his hands. Then he touches something like a
telephone, door knob, book, or computer. After he touches it
with his dirty hands, a healthy person touches the same thing

This article is continued on the next page.

---

and then touches his nose, mouth, or eyes. The germs enter our bodies in that way. **Did you get this first paragraph?**

You might be surprised to know that most people touch their nose, eyes, and mouth about three times an hour. So it's easy for germs to get inside our bodies. In order to keep from getting a cold, or in order to not give your cold to a friend, you should wash your hands often. **Understand?**

If you have a cold, you should use a paper tissue when you blow your nose, and then throw it away. Then, if possible, you should wash your hands before you touch anything like a book, pen, or telephone that other people will touch. If someone near you has a cold, you should try to wash your hands often and try not to touch your eyes, nose, or mouth. **Got it?**

B
B
B
B
B
B

Part 3
(1) Listen to Student C read the rest of the article.
(2) Using the expressions in Part 1, ask **summary clarification questions,** *even if you understand clearly.*

Part 4

Factual Questions about the article
Ask these questions and answer your partners'.

2. We catch colds from touching certain parts of our bodies with dirty hands. What parts? _____

5. How does a person with a cold get germs on their hands?
_____

8. If you don't want to get a cold from someone, what should you do often? _____

Reaction Questions about your partners' opinions and experiences. Ask these questions and ask follow-up questions.

You and the Common Cold

2. After you catch a cold, what do you do to get healthy again?
5. Tell about a time you were in a hospital.
8. Do you know anyone with bad health?

Telling Other People's Opinions and Experiences

Format: Small Groups – A, page 42; C, page 164; D, page 166

Part 1

(1) Discuss the *topics* below with your partners.

(2) Try to give details and ask questions to get more details.

(3) Listen closely to what your partners say, because in Part 2 you will tell new groups what they said.

Discussion topics

2. Tell us about a prize you won. Was it for sports, or in a contest, or at a festival?

6. Tell us about a place in your country that we should visit.

Expressions for Telling Others' Opinions and Experiences

I have no opinion about that, but I know someone who ...

I haven't, but _____ has.
                        (friend's name)

I've never done that, but my friend ...

I'm not sure, but someone told me ...

I don't know, but I do know someone who ...

B
B
B
B
B

Part 2

(1) Get into new groups.

(2) Ask your new partners the questions below. Answer their questions by telling what you learned in your first group in Part 1. Use the expressions for "Telling Others' Opinions and Experiences."

(3) ***Do not tell your own opinions or experiences***.

(4) Ask questions to get more details.

Unit 20 continues on the next page.

Telling Other People's Opinions and Experiences   **• 107**

Discussion questions

2. Have you ever won a prize?

6. What place in your country should I visit?

Part 3

(1) Discuss the *topics* below with your partners.

(2) Try to give details and ask questions to get more details.

(3) Listen closely to what your partners say, because in Part 4 you will form a new group and tell what they said.

More discussion topics

2. Tell us about something you hate.

6. Tell us about a time when you were in a hospital or very sick.

Part 4

Directions

(1) Get into new groups again.

(2) Ask your new partners the questions below. Answer their questions by telling what you learned in your second group in Part 3. Use the expressions for "Telling Others' Opinions and Experiences."

(3) ***Do not give your own opinions or experiences***.

(4) Ask questions to get more details.

More discussion questions

2. Is there anything you really hate?

6. Were you ever in a hospital or very sick?

Discussion

Format: Triads – Student A, page 44; Student C, page 168
Topic: Driving

Before Part 1 of the discussion
(1) *Silently* read your article about driving in Part 2.
(2) Write answers to your *Factual Questions* and write two more questions.
(3) Write two more *Reaction Questions* in Part 4.

Part 1
(1) Listen to Student A read the first article.
(2) Interrupt to ask clarification questions when you don't understand.
(3) Answer their *Factual Questions*.

Part 2
(1) Read this second article to your partners.
(2) Then ask your *Factual Questions*.

B
B
B
B
B
B

Teenage Drivers

More teenagers die from traffic accidents than from any other cause. Many of the teenagers who died were passengers in cars driven by other teenagers; in fact, two out of every three teenagers who die in a car accident were in cars driven by another teenager! Because of this, there is a large organization that wants to change the way teenagers get driver's licenses. It recommends that all teenagers first get a restricted driver's license, which allows them to drive with a maximum of three

This article continues on the next page.

Discussion

passengers and only during daylight hours. If, after driving with a restricted license for 18 months, a teenager has a perfect driving record (in other words, they have no tickets or accidents) and they are 18 years old, they can get a regular, unrestricted license.

Factual Questions about your article
Ask your partners these questions.

1. What's the most common cause of death for teenagers?

   _____

2. Is this sentence true or false? All teenagers who die in car accidents were in cars driven by other teenagers. _____

3. _____

4. _____

Part 3
(1) Listen to Student C read the last article.
(2) Interrupt to ask them clarification questions when you don't understand.
(3) Answer the *Factual Questions*.

Part 4

Reaction Questions about your partners' opinions and experiences. Ask these reaction questions and some follow-up questions. Write two more questions to ask. Answer your partners' questions with details.

Driver's Licenses for Teenagers

5. Is it difficult to get a driver's license in your country?
6. Do you think it is a good idea to have a restricted driver's license for teenagers?

7. _____

8. _____

Discussion   • *111*

Student B • Unit 22 ⌒

Helping the Discussion Leader Explain, I

Format: Triads – Student A, page 47; Student C, page 171

Expressions

Could you help me explain that?
Do you know what I mean?

Example

A: When I got up this morning, I felt irritable.
B: What do you mean by "irritable"?
A (to Student C): Could you help me explain that?
C (to Student B): Sure. He means he was in a bad mood. He felt cross, grumpy, and mad at the world when he got up this morning.

B
B
B
B
B
B

Part 1
(1) Student A will read some sentences to you.
(2) You ask Student A the five clarification questions below.
(3) Student A will ask Student C to help clarify the sentences for you.

1. (Student A) , what's a dentist?

2. What do you mean by "embarrassed"?

3. Sorry. I couldn't understand the question.

4. Could you give me some examples of dog tricks?

5. What does "passenger" mean?

Unit 22 continues on the next page.

Helping the Discussion Leader Explain, I

Part 2

(1) Read the following sentences to Student C.

(2) Student C will ask you to clarify, but **you don't clarify.**

(3) Ask Student A to help you explain the sentences. Try to have a brief discussion about the topic of each of these sentences.

1. (Student C) , do you know anyone who's a good athlete?
    After Student B's clarification question:
    (Student A) , do you know what I mean?

2. When I was younger, I always wanted my parents to get me a pet.

3. Usually, right before I take a trip abroad, I feel a lot of stress.

4. Do you think both spouses in a marriage should share the housework?

5. Have you ever felt homesick?

Part 3

(1) Student C will read some sentences to Student A.

(2) Student A will ask Student C clarification questions.

(3) Student C will ask you to help clarify for Student A. Help Student C explain. Try to have a brief discussion about the topic of each sentence.

B
B
B
B
B
B

Student B • Unit 23 ⌒

Helping the Discussion
Leader Explain, II

Format: Triads – Student A, page 49; Student C, page 173
Topic: Part 1. Fathers Who Live Longer
         Part 2. Smoking and Aging
         Part 3. Tasting Foods

Before Part 1 of the discussion
(1) *Silently* read your article about smoking and aging in Part 2.
(2) Write answers to your *Factual Questions* and write two more questions.
(3) Write two more *Reaction Questions* in Part 4.

Part 1
(1) Listen to Student A read the first article.
(2) For practice, ask **clarification questions**, *even if you understand clearly.*

Part 2
(1) Read this article to your partners.
(2) Don't answer your partners' clarification questions.
(3) Ask a partner to help you explain.
(4) Try to use the **"Help the Leader" Expressions.**
(5) Ask your *Factual Questions.*

"Help the Leader"
Expressions

Could you help me explain that?
Do you know what I mean?

Unit 23 continues on the next page.

Smoking and Aging

This article discusses the effect that smoking has on people. Researchers were interested in finding out if smoking caused a person to age faster; in other words, if they look older faster. So they studied identical twins, because identical twins have the same genes; this means that they should age at the same rate, unless something on the outside causes one of them to age faster. **Understand?**

The researchers found 50 sets of twins in which one twin was a nonsmoker and the other a life-long smoker. They found that the smoking twin had skin that was 25% thinner than the nonsmoker. The reason that this is interesting is because thinner skin gets more wrinkles. As a result, the smoking twins had more wrinkles. **Did you understand that part?**

The researchers also found that there's a connection between smoking and gray hair and baldness. Surprisingly, 88% of smokers either were bald or had gray hair; on the other hand, only 68% of nonsmokers were bald or had gray hair. **OK?**

B
B
B
B
B
B

Unit 23 continues on the next page.

Factual Questions about the article

Ask these questions about the article.

1. _____

2. Why should identical twins age at the same rate?

_____

3. Is this true or false? The nonsmokers had fewer wrinkles than the smokers.

_____

4. _____

Part 3

(1) Listen to Student C read the last article.

(2) For practice, ask **clarification questions**, *even if you understand clearly.*

Part 4

Reaction Questions about your partners' opinions and experiences

5. About the article on smoking and aging, were you surprised to learn that people who smoke look older than people who don't smoke?

6. Do you know any pairs of twins? If so, do they look the same age?

7. _____

8. _____

Discussion

Format: Triads – Student A, page 52; Student C, page 176
Topic: Gambling

Before Part 1 of the discussion
(1) *Silently* read your part of the article about gambling
    in Part 2.
(2) Write answers to your *Factual Questions* and write two
    more questions.

Part 1
(1) Listen to Student A read the first part of this article.
(2) Interrupt to ask clarification questions when you don't
    understand.
(3) Answer their *Factual Questions*.

Part 2
(1) Read this second part of the article to your partners.
(2) Then ask them your *Factual Questions*.

B
B
B
B
B
B

Gambling (B)

Compulsive gambling is a psychological problem. Experts say
that about 5% of the people who try to gamble lose control and
develop serious problems. Most people who try to gamble and
start to lose money understand that they should quit. However,
when the compulsive gamblers start to lose, they decide to
gamble more; they think the solution to their problem is to
improve their gambling. Unfortunately, sometimes even
average people can become compulsive gamblers.

Nowadays, many states in the U.S. have lotteries, and New
York State has a typical one. In the New York lottery, a
person can buy a ticket with six numbers on it for $1.00.

This article continues on page 119.

Discussion   **• 117**

Discussion

If some of the numbers are chosen, the person wins some money, but if all six of the numbers are chosen, it is possible to win a lot of money. Some lottery winners have won over a million dollars!

Factual Questions about your article
Ask your partners these questions.

1. _____

2. Is this true or false? When compulsive gamblers start to lose money, they decide to quit gambling.

_____

3. Please explain about the New York lottery.

_____

4. _____

Part 3
   (1) Listen to Student C read the last part of the article.
   (2) Interrupt to ask clarification questions when you don't understand.
   (3) Answer the *Factual Questions*.

Part 4

Reaction Questions about your partners' opinions and experiences. Ask the questions below and some follow-up questions. Answer your partners' questions with details.

Lady Luck and You

2. What things give you a lot of energy and excitement?
   For example: a. gambling   b. sports   c. music
   d. computer games   e. traveling   f. doing something dangerous, like driving a motorcycle fast   g. other

5. Do you sometimes have fantasies about being rich?

   (Think of two more *Reaction Questions* about gambling.)

Discussion

Expressing Opinions, I

Format: Pairs – Student A, page 55
Topic: Information from a Survey

Part 1: Survey
   (1) Ask five or more people these questions.
   (2) Mark their choices on the chart.

Question	*Number*	*Question*	*Number*
1. What do you most enjoy doing during free time?		**6. How often do you feel stress in this school?**	
a. watching TV		a. often	
b. playing sports or exercising		b. sometimes	
c. reading books or magazines		c. rarely	
2. Where is the best place to study?		**7. Do you try to get exercise every day?**	
a. library			
b. bedroom		a. Yes	
c. lounge		b. No	
3. Do you want to live in your hometown in the future?		**8. Which do you feel is better: married life or single life?**	
a. yes		a. married life	
b. no		b. single life	
4. What is the perfect number of children to have?		**9. In high school, which subject did you enjoy the most?**	
a. none		a. math	
b. 1		b. science	
c. 2		c. languages	
d. more than 2		d. history	
5. Have you smoked a cigarette at least once?		**10. Are you shy?**	
a. yes		a. yes	
b. no		b. no	

Before Part 2 of the discussion

Silently read the sentences in Part 2 and choose an answer.

Part 2

    (1) Read these sentences to your partner.
    (2) Discuss your opinions.

1. In my opinion, most people think women should get married at _____ years old.
     a. 20 – 23
     b. 24 – 26
     c. 27 or older
2. I think most people feel watching TV is _____.
     a. a waste of time
     b. an important use of time
3. I feel sure most people _____ a serious problem at this time.
     a. are having
     b. aren't having
4. I'd bet that most people _____ .
     a. like summer better than winter
     b. like winter better than summer
5. About blood types, don't you think most people would say ____?
     a. they have type A
     b. they have type B
     c. they have type AB
     d. they have type O
     e. they don't know what type they are
6. I believe most people like to vacation _____.
     a. at a beach resort
     b. at a mountain resort
     c. in a famous city
7. I think most people ____ uncomfortable around foreigners.
     a. feel
     b. don't feel

B
B
B
B
B
B

Unit 25 continues on the next page.

Expressing Opinions, I

8. Regarding movies, I think most people prefer to watch _____.
   a. comedy
   b. mystery
   c. adventure
9. I imagine most people _____ coffee every day.
   a. drink
   b. don't drink
10. I feel sure most people like to watch _____ .
    a. tennis
    b. soccer
    c. basketball
    d. baseball

Part 3
   (1) Listen to your partner give some opinions.
   (2) Referring to your survey, agree or disagree with your partner using the expressions below.
   (3) Discuss your own opinions.

B
B
B
B
B
B

Expressions for Agreeing

Yes, you're right. I found that most people ...
I agree. I learned that most people ...
You've got it right. Most people in my survey ...

Expressions for Disagreeing

I'm afraid I disagree. I found that most people ...
Are you sure? Actually, I learned that most people ...
It's interesting. I found something different. Most ...

Expressing Opinions, II

Format: Small Groups – A, page 58; C, page 179; D, page 182
Topics: Part 1.   The Rights of Mothers and Fathers
Part 2.   Death Caused by Cigarettes
Part 3.   De-barking Dogs
Part 4.   63-year-old Woman Has a Baby

Agreeing

That's a good point.
I totally agree with _____.
That's right.

Disagreeing

I'm afraid I disagree.
That's a good point, but . . .
Actually, I think . . .

B
B
B
B
B
B

Before Part 1 of the discussion
Silently read this article about death and cigarettes
in Part 2.

Part 1
(1)   Listen to Student A read the first article.
(2)   Answer and discuss the questions.

Part 2
(1)   Read your article to your partners.
(2)   Then ask the *Factual* and *Reaction Questions*.

Unit 26 continues on the next page.

Death Caused by Cigarettes

Fifty years ago, when Jean Conner was a teenager, she started smoking cigarettes. She said she started smoking after seeing ads in magazines of beautiful models smoking and after watching famous movie stars smoking in movies. She thought smoking was glamorous. As she got older, she began to smoke more and more; soon she was smoking three packs a day. That means she smoked 60 cigarettes a day. At the age of 45 she quit smoking, but a month later she found out that she had cancer. She died four years later.

Now Jean Conner's daughter is suing the tobacco company; she wants the cigarette maker to pay her money because, she says, cigarettes caused her mother's death. According to the daughter, cigarettes are addictive, and cigarette companies try to make people start smoking and become addicted to tobacco. She also said that her mother started smoking before there were warnings on cigarette packs telling people that tobacco might cause health problems. She said cigarettes cause thousands of people to die every year. The

This article is continued on the next page.

       Expressing Opinions, II

tobacco company, on the other hand, says that they should not have to pay money to the daughter. The company says that people choose whether to smoke or not; cigarette companies don't force people to smoke. The company also says that even though Jean Conner knew there were health risks, she continued to smoke. Furthermore, the company said that Jean Conner was not addicted to cigarettes, because she was able to stop smoking at age 45 and 50 million other Americans have quit smoking, too.

Factual Questions about the article

Ask these questions about the article.

1. Why does the daughter think that the cigarette company should pay?
2. Why does the cigarette company think that it shouldn't have to pay?

Reaction Questions about your partners' opinions. Ask these questions about the article. Agree or disagree with your partners. Express your own opinions as well.

Curing the World of Cigarettes

1. Who do you agree with, the daughter or the tobacco company?
2. Do you think cigarettes should be illegal, like marijuana and other drugs? Would that stop people in your country and all over the world from smoking? What will stop them?

Parts 3 & 4

1. Listen to Students C & D read their articles.
2. Answer and discuss their questions.

Referring to a Source

Format: Triads – Student A, page 61; Student C, page 185
Topic: Bullying

┌─── **Referring to a Source** ───┐

I read that _____.
I heard that _____.
According to an article I read, _____.
According to the newspaper, _____.

└──────────────────────────────┘

Before Part 1 of the discussion
(1) *Silently* read the information from the article about bullying.
(2) **Do not read this article to your partners.**

B
B
B
B
B
B

Bullying (B)

This article about bullying explains why bullies pick on other kids, why they hurt other kids.

Usually, bullies are not aware of the feelings of others. They tend to think other kids are trying to annoy them or make them angry, even when they really aren't. Bullies feel that they have the right to react and hurt the other kids. Also, bullies usually have been victims of other bullies, so they learn to be violent from their own experience as victims; they believe aggression is the best solution to their problems.

Bullies also feel a great need to belong to a group. Bullies often have two or three friends who are also aggressive kids. They find that their friends admire physical strength, so one

This article is continued on the next page.

way for them to impress their friends is to pick on weaker kids. One girl said she bullied others because her friends did it, too. Another girl said she was afraid that if she didn't bully someone, her friends might bully her.

Finally, some kids bully others because they feel a kind of excitement when hurting others.
Source: Japan Times

Part 1

Answer Student A's questions by giving your opinions. You don't have to refer to a source.

Part 2

(1) Don't read this article to your partners.
(2) Instead, ask the following question.
(3) After your partners answer, tell them what you have learned from the article. Don't read it to them.
(4) Try to use the expressions for **"Referring to a Source."**

A question for your partners

Why do you think bullies pick on and hurt other kids?

Part 3

Answer Student C's questions by giving your opinions. You don't have to refer to a source.

Part 4

Discussion about your partners' opinions and experiences with bullying

Ask your partners these questions and answer their questions.

2. When you were younger, did you feel that you were different from other kids?
5. When you were younger, if someone was bullying you, how did you react?

Referring to a Source • *127*

Summary Discussion

Format: Triads – Student A, page 64; Student C, page 187
Topics: Part 1. Best Friends
        Part 2. The Effects of Watching TV
        Part 3. Spanking

Before Part 1 of the discussion
  (1) Review the Discussion Strategies with your partner(s).
  (2) First, fill in the blanks in the Summary box below by
      asking each other for examples.
  (3) Then go back to the unit where the strategy is introduced to
      review other phrases and expressions.
  (4) Then *silently* read your article in Part 1.

Discussion Strategies Summary

Rejoinders (Unit 1)	_____
Follow-up Questions (Unit 1)	*What movie did you see?*
Clarification Expressions (Unit 2)	_____
Comprehension Checks (Unit 3)	_____
Answering with Details (Unit 5)	*and, so, but, because*
Interrupting (Unit 12)	_____
Words That Describe (Unit 13)	_____
Telling What You've Heard (Unit 15)	*B said (that) . . .*
Volunteering an Answer (Unit 16)	_____
Summary Clarification Questions (Unit 19)	_____
Telling Others' Opinions (Unit 20)	*I know someone who. . .*
Helping the Leader (Unit 22)	_____
Expressing Opinions (Unit 25)	_____
Referring to a Source (Unit 27)	*According to . . .*

B B B B B B

Part 1

   (1) Listen to Student A read the first article.

   (2) Then discuss it with your partners, using discussion strategies.

Part 2

   (1) Read this article to your partners.

   (2) Then discuss it, using the strategies above.

The Effects of Watching TV

This article tells about some problems that are caused by watching TV. There's a town in Canada that didn't have TV until only 20 years ago. Researchers compared the people in that town to people in two towns that had had TV for 40 years. They found that people who watch a lot of TV are not as creative as people who don't watch much. For example, the researchers gave some problem-solving tests to children. The children who didn't watch much TV had more ideas about how to solve the problems than children who watched a lot. They were also faster at thinking of ideas.

Researchers explained the reason why people who do not watch a lot of TV are more creative. To be creative, you need to become bored. When some people get bored, they just watch TV. They aren't active. When other people get bored, they start to think of ways to entertain themselves. They become active and creative. For example, they play

This article is continued on the next page.

          Summary Discussion

games, paint pictures, write letters, or go for a walk. Sometimes they seek out a friend to spend time with, a friend who enjoys socializing and doesn't want to watch TV. Every time these people start to get bored, they find creative and healthy ways to amuse themselves. In summary, if you want to be a creative person, it's a good idea *not* to watch TV when you get bored.

Part 3
    (1) Listen to Student C read the last article.
    (2) Then discuss it with your partners, using discussion strategies.

Part 4

Discuss your discussion

    (1) Did you use a lot of the strategies you've been practicing?
    (2) Which ones did you use?
        Which ones didn't you use? Why not?

B
B
B
B
B
B

┌ **Rejoinders** ┐	┌ **Follow-up Questions** ┐
I see.	*(Questions about an answer)*
Oh, yeah?	**A: What did you do last night?**
Really?	**B: I watched a movie on TV.**
That's great!	**A:** *(Rejoinder and Follow-up)* **I see.**
That's too bad.	**What movie did you watch?**

Format: Triads – Student A, page 1; Student B, page 67

Before the discussion

(1) ***Silently*** read and answer the questions below for yourself, but ***do not write the answers***.

(2) Write two more questions about any topic.

Discussion Directions

(1) Ask *both* of your partners your discussion questions.

(2) After they answer, ask **follow-up questions** and use **rejoinders**.

(3) Take turns. Student A begins with question #1. Student B asks #2, then you ask #3, and you continue.

(4) Answer their questions with details by using ***and, but, so, because,*** or **two sentences** each time you answer.

Discussion Questions

3. Have you ever had _____?

6. Would you like to _____?

9. What are you most worried about _____?

12. Do you know how to _____?

15. Is/Are _____ important to you?

18. What is most important for a job, salary, vacation, or high status?

21. _____?

24. _____?

Note: Follow-up questions frequently use WH-questions.

What movie?	Where did you see it?
Who was in it?	Why did you choose that one?
What did you think of it?	How long was it?
How often do you go to the movies?	

Rejoinders and Follow-up Questions   **• 133**

Student C • Unit 5 ⌒

Answering with Details

Format: Triads – Student A, page 9; Student B, page 75

Before the discussion
   (1) *Silently* read and answer the questions below for yourself, but *do not write the answers*.
   (2) Write two more questions about any topic.

Discussion Directions
   (1) Ask these questions of *both* of your partners.
   (2) After they answer, ask them follow-up questions.
   (3) Answer their questions *with details* by using **and, but, so, because,** or **two sentences** each time you answer.

Discussion Questions

Some Personal Questions

3. How often do you use a cell phone every day?

6. Do all the members of your family usually eat dinner together?

9. How is your health recently?

12. How is your generation different from your parents' generation?

15. If I were coming to your house for dinner tonight, what would you make for me ?

18. What makes you to feel nervous?

21. _____?

24. _____?

Discussion

Format: Triads – Student A, page 11; Student B, page 77
Topic: Your High School Days

Before the discussion
(1) *Silently* read the questions below, but *do not write* the answers.
(2) Write two more questions about the topic.

Discussion Directions
(1) Ask these questions of *both* of your partners.
(2) After they answer, ask them **follow-up questions**, and use **rejoinders** (e.g. ,"I see," "That's too bad," or "That's great!").
    [Note: "e.g." is an academic abbreviation meaning "for example."]
(3) Also, answer your partners' questions *with details*.

Discussion Questions

Your High School Days
3. Was your school co-educational (both boys and girls)?
6. Do you wish you could have gone to a different school?
9. Did you have any friends of the opposite sex, or were your friends the same sex as you?
12. What kinds of things did you enjoy doing in your free time?
15. Were your school rules strict?
18. Were you ever scolded by a teacher?
21. Did your school have special parties, festivals, or other events?
24. Did you have to take any special exams in order to enter your high school or to graduate?
27. Were you allowed to have cell phones in your school?
30. Which subjects did you hate?
33. What was the most difficult thing for you in those days?
36. _____

C
C
C
C
C
C

CCCCC

Paragraph Clarifications, I

Focus: Paragraph-by-paragraph clarifications, with clarification questions provided

Format: Triads – Student A, page 12; Student B, page 78

Topic: Animals in Movies

Before Part 1 of the discussion

(1) *Silently* read your part of the article (C) about animals in movies in Part 3.

(2) Write the answers to the *Factual Questions* in Part 4.

Parts 1 & 2

Listen to Students A & B tell their parts of the story. *After each paragraph*, ask the appropriate **clarification question** below.

PARAGRAPH 1: Did you say a person was killed in a movie?

PARAGRAPH 2: What did you say "AHS" means?

PARAGRAPH 3: Did you say some people were angry? At whom? Why?

PARAGRAPH 4: Did you say the horses are never hurt? Why (not)?

PARAGRAPH 5: Can you explain again what electronic animals are?

PARAGRAPH 6: I don't understand the word "parachutes."

Part 3

(1) Read this third part of the story to your partners.

(2) *Stop after each paragraph* to ask your **comprehension check**.

(3) Then answer your partners' **clarification questions**.

Animals in Movies (C)

7. We'll continue with the last part of this story. This is paragraph 7. When animals are used in movies, the AHS comes to the movie set and watches the animals closely, because movie-making can be stressful for animals. Lions and tigers become irritable, or short-tempered, if they have to wait a long time for their scene. Elephants will sway, in other words, move back and forth, when they feel stress.

Do you understand paragraph 7?

This article is continued on the next page.

Paragraph Clarifications, I

C
C
C
C
C
C

8. In one movie, they used 50 fish. They needed these fish for 4 days. The AHS made sure that the fish had clean water every day and that the water temperature was correct, in other words, not too hot or too cold.
   ### Understand the eighth paragraph?

9. The AHS watches every animal in a movie: lions, bears, elephants, dogs, and even bugs (which are insects). For example, the actors in a movie aren't allowed to hurt or kill even cockroaches.
   ### OK?

Part 4

Factual Questions about the story
Ask your partners the following questions.

9. Why do movie animals sometimes feel stress?

_____

10. What did the AHS do about the 50 fish that were in a movie?

_____

11. What are some animals that are used in movies?

_____

12. What's a cockroach?

_____

Reaction Questions about your partners' opinions and experiences. Ask these questions and ask follow-up questions.

You, Animals, and the Movies

3. In your country, are people sometimes cruel to animals? Explain.
6. How much does it cost to rent a video in your country?
9. Which do you prefer, foreign-made movies or movies made in your own country?
12. (Think of some questions about this topic of movies and animals.)

Paragraph Clarifications, II

Focus: Paragraph-by-paragraph clarifications, clarification
questions *not* provided
Format: **Triads** – Student A, page 14; Student B, page 80
Topic: Sleep

Before Part 1 of the discussion

  (1) *Silently* read your part (C) of the article about sleep in Part 3.
  (2) Write the answers to the *Factual Questions* about the article.

Parts 1 & 2

  (1) Listen to your partners read the rest of the article.
  (2) When they ask if you understand, ask your own
     clarification questions, *even if you understand clearly.*

Part 3

  (1) Read this third part of the story to your partners.
  (2) *Stop after each paragraph* to ask your **comprehension check.**
  (3) Answer your partners' **clarification questions.**
  (4) Then ask your partners your *Factual Questions.*

Sleep (C)

7. Here is some more advice for good sleep habits. You should get
physical exercise every day. If you exercise, you'll get a
deeper sleep and you won't need as much sleep.
   Do you understand that paragraph?

8. Next, if you often have trouble sleeping, you should take a hot
bath before going to bed, or read a book for pleasure. Also, you
should be sure your bedroom is quiet, dark, and cool. If you go to
bed and cannot fall asleep within 20 minutes, you should get up
and do something else until you're sleepy.
   Got it?

This news story is continued on the next page.

C
C
C
C
C
C

9. The final piece of advice is about caffeine. You shouldn't drink coffee or tea if you feel sleepy in the middle of the day. Instead of a coffee break, it's better if you take a nap. A 15- to 20-minute nap is very helpful. However, you should not take a nap for more than 20 minutes. If your nap is too long, you'll fall into a deep sleep and you'll feel even more tired when you wake up. **Understand?**

Factual Questions about the article

1. Regarding sleep, what are two good effects that you get from doing physical exercise?

_____

2. If you have trouble sleeping, what are two things you can do?

_____

3. What should you do if you can't fall asleep after 20 minutes?

_____

4. If you get sleepy in the middle of the day, which is better for you, to drink some coffee or to take a nap?

_____

5. Is it good to take a nap for an hour? Why (not)?

_____

6. What happens if your nap is too long?

_____

Part 4

Reaction Questions about your partners' opinions and experiences. Ask these questions and ask follow-up questions.

Sleeping Habits

3. Do you sometimes fall asleep while watching movies or TV, or while reading a book?
6. Are you a deep sleeper or light sleeper? (In other words, do you wake up easily if there is noise?)
9. Do you know anyone who doesn't sleep enough?
12. Do you drink or eat when you feel sleepy during the day?
15. (Think of two more questions about **sleep** and ask your partners.)

C
C
C
C
C
C

Paragraph Clarifications, II

Unit 9 • Student C

— Asking for More Details —

Could you give me an example of _____?
What do you mean _____?
Could you explain _____?
Could you tell me why/who/what _____?
I'd like to know more about _____.

Format: Triads – Student A, page 16; Student B, page 82

Before the discussion
(1) *Silently* read the sentences below and fill in the blanks.

Discussion Directions
(1) Read these sentences to your partners.
(2) Listen to your partners' sentences. **Ask them for more details**.

Discussion Starters

3. If you were a doctor or psychiatrist, I would ask you for advice about _____

6. When I'm 65 years old,_____

9. _____ is the person I would like to have dinner with some day.

12. There are two main reasons why I'm glad I'm _____: First, _____ _____ And second, _____

15. One thing I hope I never have to do is _____

18. As a child, my favorite toy was _____

C
C
C
C
C
C

Asking for More Details • *141*

Student C • Unit 10 ⌒

Discussion

Format: Triads – Student A, page 17; Student B, page 83
Topic: Stress

Before Part 1 of the discussion
(1) **Silently** read your part (C) of the article about stress in Part 3.
(2) Write answers to your *Factual Questions* and then write two more questions.

Parts 1 & 2
(1) Listen to your partners read the first and second parts of the article.
(2) Ask clarification questions when you don't understand.
(3) Answer the *Factual Questions* they ask you.

Part 3
(1) Read this last part of the article (C) to your partners.
(2) Answer any clarification questions they have.
(3) Ask them your *Factual Questions*.

Stress (C)

This is the third part of the article. It is not important that you have a lot of friends. It is important that you have close friends, even if you have only a few. **Understand?** For your health, the most important relationships are with the people whom you see every day, for example, roommates or romantic partners. In a study, the happier roommates were, the healthier they were. When roommates felt stress because they disliked each other, they got more colds and the flu. **Do you understand the word "flu"?** The relationship between romantic partners is deeper than that between roommates, and the statistics showed romantic relations, both good and bad, had a greater effect on health.

This article is continued on page 144.

C
C
C
C
C
C

Discussion

The friendliest monkeys were the healthiest

Researchers also studied the effect of relationships and stress on heart disease. **OK?** They found that monkeys that were not friendly had more heart disease. They also studied 195 elderly people who had had heart attacks. They found that a year after having their heart attacks elderly people who had close friends and relatives were twice as likely to be alive as elderly people who had no such relationships. **Understand? Do you want me to explain that again?** For example, some of the older people said they had two or more friends; only 27% of them died within the first year. But for those elderly people who said they had no friends, 58% died within the first year after having a heart attack. **Do you understand?**

Factual Questions about the article

1. Which is more important for health: to have a lot of friends, or to have a few close friends? _____

2. What happened to the health of roommates who disliked each other? _____

3. _____

4. _____

Part 4

Reaction Questions about your partners' opinions and experiences. Ask the questions below and ask follow-up questions. Also, answer your partners' questions with details.

Stress in Our Lives

3. If you feel stress, do you get sick (for example, get a cold or flu)?

6. What are some things that cause stress for people in your country?

(Think of two more *Reaction Questions*.)

C
C
C
C
C
C

Discussion

Discussion

Format: Triads – Student A, page 21; Student B, page 87
Topic: Your Hometown and Childhood Home

Before the discussion
   (1) *Silently* read the discussion questions below, but ***do not write*** the answers.
   (2) Write two more questions about the topic of your hometown and childhood home.

Discussion directions
   (1) Ask *both of* your partners your discussion questions.
   (2) Try to use these *discussion strategies*.

── Discussion Strategies ──

Ask **follow-up questions** and **solicit more details.**
  (e.g., "Could you give me an example?" "What do you mean____?" or "Could you explain _____?")
Use **rejoinders.**
  (e.g., "I see," "That's too bad," or "That's great!")
Answer questions **with details.**
  (e.g., answer with *and, but, so, because,* or with *two sentences.)*

Discussion Questions

Your Hometown and Childhood Home

3. Does your hometown have many foreigners?
6. If we visited your hometown together, what would we do?
9. When you're away from your hometown, do you feel homesick?
12. Please describe your bedroom with as many details as possible.
15. If you were going to build a house for yourself, would it be different from your childhood home?
18. Did people in your neighborhood recycle things, for example, newspapers, cans, and bottles?

21. _____

24. _____

C
C
C
C
C
C

Student C • Unit 12 ⌒

┌─ Interrupting Someone ─┐

Excuse me. Could I ask something?
Uhh, sorry for interrupting, but . . .
Excuse me, but I have a question.

Format: Triads – Student A, page 22; Student B, page 88
Topic: Telling Lies

Before Part 1 of the discussion

(1) **Silently** read your part (C) of the article about telling lies in Part 3.

(2) Write answers to your *Factual Questions* about the article .

Part 1

(1) Listen to Student A read the first part of the article.

(2) Interrupt *while* A is reading and ask some **clarification questions** *even if you understand clearly.*

(3) Try to use the **"Interrupting Someone"** expressions.

For example: Uhh, sorry for interrupting, (use A's name) , but I have a question. Could you explain again why a worker will lie to the boss?

Part 2

Listen to Student B, interrupt, and ask clarification questions. Use the **"Interrupting Someone"** expressions.

For example: Excuse me, (use B's name) . I have a question. Why do people tell self-centered lies?

Unit 12 is continued on the next page.

C
C
C
C
C
C

Interrupting Someone

Part 3

   (1) Read this third part of the article (C) to your partners.

   (2) ***Don't ask them if they understand***, but answer their clarification questions when they interrupt you.

   (3) When you're finished, ask them your *Factual Questions*.

Telling Lies (C)

Accphording to our research, extroverts tell more lies than introverts.Extroverts are people who like to spend a lot of time talking with other people. Introverts are people who prefer quiet time alone reading or with just one or two other people. Introverts tell fewer lies than extroverts. Our reasearch also found that people who worry about what others think of them tell more lies than those who don't.

Here's some other information we learned from the research. People don't think small lies are serious, they don't usually plan in advance to tell lies, and most people don't worry about getting caught telling a lie.

After doing our research, however, we believe that some lies are serious. For example, let's say you want to sell your car, which has a problem with its engine. In order to sell it at a high price, you might tell a lie by saying that your car has no problems. In this case, you influenced someone to do something by telling a lie. That is a serious lie.

Finally, our research suggests that being honest all the time *isn't* a good idea. When we insist on telling the truth, we can hurt other people's feelings. If we were always completely honest, we might not have many friends.

C
C
C
C
C
C

Unit 12 is continued on the next page.

Interrupting Someone

Factual Questions about the article

1. What do you call people who talk a lot with other people?

   _____

2. Who tells more lies, introverts or extroverts?

   _____

3. Do people usually plan to tell lies in advance?

   _____

4. Was the example about selling a car with a bad engine an example of a little lie or a serious lie?

   _____

5. Why are lies sometimes a good idea?

   _____

Part 4

Reaction Questions about your partners' opinions and experiences. Ask these questions and follow-up questions.

To Lie or Not to Lie

3. Let's say you're renting an apartment. One day, you accidentally make a hole in the wall. The landlord says it will cost $30 to fix. Would you tell the landlord the truth, or would you say that the hole was already there?

6. If you wanted to sell something (for example, a car, a CD player, or a bike) but you knew there was a small problem with it, would you tell a person who was interested in buying it?

9. What polite lie have you told recently?

12. Do you worry about people lying to you? If so, in what kind of situation?

C
C
C
C
C
C

Interrupting Someone

Words That Describe

```
┌─────────────── Expressions ───────────────┐
│                                            │
│   It is a person/animal/place/thing that ___. │
│   It is an event/condition/situation that ____. │
│   It is a type/kind/sort of ____.          │
│   You can find it at/in ____.              │
│                                            │
└────────────────────────────────────────────┘
```

Format: Triads – Student A, page 25; Student B, page 91

Before starting
   (1) *Silently* look the words in the list below.
   (2) *Don't show or tell your words to your partners.*

Directions
   (1) Take turns. Using the expressions above, describe your words to your partners.
   (2) Don't say the word.
   (3) They will try to guess the word.
   (4) If they cannot guess the word, they can ask a question.

museum	DVD	Olympics	mosquito
computer mouse		extrovert	barefoot
nap	dream	cockroach	flu
jogging	psychiatrist		

C
C
C
C
C
C

Dropping a butter knife during a meal means a male visitor is forthcoming

Discussion

Format: Triads – Student A, page 27; Student B, page 93
Topic: Superstitions

Before Part 1 of the discussion

(1) *Silently* read your part of the article (C) in Part 3 below.
(2) Write answers to the *Factual Questions* and write two more questions.

Parts 1 & 2

(1) Listen to your partners read the first and second parts of the article.
(2) *Interrupt and ask clarification questions* when you don't understand.
(3) Answer your partners' *Factual Questions.*

Part 3

(1) Read this last part of the article to your partners.
(2) Then ask your *Factual Questions.*

Superstitions (c)

According to experts who study Russian culture, there is a reason why Russians have become more serious about traditional superstitions. After the communist system ended some years ago, there was instability in Russia; people began looking for something that they could believe in. For this reason, Russians became more interested in traditional religions and superstitions. **Is that clear?**

Although belief in superstitions seems strongest among old people and people in the countryside, experts say that we can find it everywhere in Russian society. For example, shaking hands in a doorway is considered bad luck by even some educated Russians. There's an interesting example of this concerning a Russian cosmonaut. The cosmonaut was

This article is continued on the next page.

Discussion

C
C
C
C
C

on the Russian space station when it connected with the American space shuttle. After the space station and space shuttle joined, a door between the two was opened and the American astronaut reached out (or extended) his hand through the doorway to greet the Russians with a handshake. As we know, Russians generally believe shaking hands through a doorway is bad luck, so, at first, the cosmonaut would not do it. However, after a few moments' hesitation, he decided to shake hands anyway even though it might be risky. **Understand?**

Factual Questions about the article

1. What caused Russians to begin looking for something that they could believe in?

   _____

2. Who seems to believe in superstitions the most?

   _____

3. _____

4. _____

Reaction Questions about your partners' opinions and experiences

(1) Ask these questions and then follow-up questions.
(2) Answer your partners' questions with details.

It's Your Lucky Day

3. Do you know anyone who is superstitious?
6. Have you had any experiences with good or bad luck because of something you did?

(Think of two more *Reaction Questions* about superstitions.)

Telling What You've Heard

```
┌─        Phrases for Telling        ─┐
          A told me about . . . .
          B said (that) . . . .
          C told me (that) . . . .
          B explained (that) . . . .
          According to A, . . . .
└                                     ┘
```

Format: Triads – Student A, page 29; Student B, page 95

Topics: Part 1. Short People Live Longer

Part 2. Gossiping

Part 3. Why the French Have Fewer Heart Attacks

Before the discussion

(1) *Silently* read your article in Part 3.

(2) Write the answers to the *Factual Questions* about the article.

Part 1

(1) Leave your group and sit in a different part of the room. *Do not listen* to Student A's article.

(2) After Student A tells Student B about the article, come back to the group. Student B will explain the article to you.

(3) Answer Student A's *Factual Questions* about the article.

Part 2

(1) Listen to Student B tell you about the article, "Gossiping." ***Don't take notes.***

(2) Tell Student A about the article.

(3) Student A will answer Student B's *Factual Questions* about the article. ***Don't answer or help.***

Part 3

(1) Tell Student A about your article, "Why the French Have Fewer Heart Attacks."

(2) Do *not* tell Student B.

(3) Student A will tell B what they heard about the article.

(4) Then you ask Student B your *Factual Questions* below.

Unit 15 is continued on the next page.

C
C
C
C
C
C

Why the French Have Fewer Heart Attacks

Many people are surprised to learn that French people have fewer heart attacks than people in many other countries. When we think of French food, we often imagine sauces that have a lot of fat in them. Some scientists think the reason why the French have fewer heart attacks is that they drink wine with their meals. However, there may be another reason why they have fewer heart attacks.

Researchers studied the diets of 40 countries. They found that the French eat a lot of vegetables, compared to people in other countries. For example, people in Finland drink a lot of milk and eat a lot of dairy products, like eggs and cheese. But Finns don't eat as many vegetables. Researchers found that the Finns had more heart attacks than the French; in fact, the Finns had five times as many heart attacks as the French.

So the researchers say that eating a lot of vegetables is very good for our health. And they warn that, if we drink wine, we shouldn't drink too much. They say that eating extra carrots isn't dangerous, but drinking an extra glass of wine might be.

Unit 15 is continued on the next page.

C
C
C
C
C
C

Telling What You've Heard

Factual Questions about the article, "Why the French Have Fewer Heart Attacks"

1. Is this true or false? French people have more heart attacks than other Europeans. _____

2. What do the French drink with meals?

   _____

3. What do the French eat a lot of?

   _____

4. Why do people in Finland have a lot of heart attacks?

   _____

5. Finns had how many times more heart attacks than the French? _____

6. Which is safer, drinking an extra glass of wine or eating extra carrots? _____

Part 4

Reaction Questions about your partners' opinions and experiences. Discussion about the article, "Why the French Have Fewer Heart Attacks"

Your Feelings about Eating a Healthy Diet

11. Do you feel that you have a healthy diet?
12. How many times a day do you eat vegetables?
13. What's your favorite food?
14. What types of food do you dislike?
15. Have you ever eaten French food? Chinese? Italian? Thai? Turkish? Mexican?

C
C
C
C
C
C

Volunteering an Answer

┌ Phrases for Volunteering ┐

I think (that) . . .
In my opinion, . . .
I'd like to say (that) . . .
May I say (that) . . .?
Can I answer that?
Can I respond to that?

Format: Small Groups – A, p. 32; B, p. 98; D, p. 157; E, p.158

Directions for Asking

(1) Ask your questions below in any order.

(2) ***Do not ask anyone directly.*** (In other words, don't look at anyone or say anyone's name.)

(3) Your partners will volunteer to answer.

Directions for Volunteering

(1) ***Volunteer to answer*** your partners' questions ***with details.*** (Answer with **and, but, so, because,** or **two sentences.**)

(2) Try to answer first sometimes, and sometimes wait for your partners to volunteer.

(3) Ask follow-up questions, too.

Questions for volunteers to answer

- Do you have a lucky or favorite number?
- What's the most beautiful place in your country?
- Did you have a hobby as a child?
- What is your favorite website?
- If you bought a car today, what color would you choose?
- (You think of some questions.)

Volunteering an Answer

Volunteering an Answer

Phrases for Volunteering

I think (that) . . .
In my opinion, . . .
I'd like to say (that) . . .
May I say (that) . . .?
Can I answer that?
Can I respond to that?

Format: Small Groups – A, p. 32; B, p. 98; C, p. 156; E, p. 158

Directions for Asking

(1) Ask your questions below in any order.

(2) ***Do not ask anyone directly.*** (In other words, don't look at anyone or say anyone's name.)

(3) Your partners will volunteer to answer.

Directions for Volunteering

(1) ***Volunteer to answer*** your partners' questions ***with details.*** (Answer with **and, but, so, because,** or **two sentences**.)

(2) Try to answer first sometimes, and sometimes wait for your partners to volunteer.

(3) Ask follow-up questions, too.

Questions for volunteers to answer

- Which do you prefer: team sports like basketball or individual sports like tennis?
- Did your computer ever get a virus?
- What company would you like to work for?
- If you have trouble falling asleep, what do you do?
- What's the most expensive thing you own?
- (You think of some questions.)

D
D
D
D
D

Student E • Unit 16 ⌒∽

Volunteering an Answer

```
┌─ Phrases for Volunteering ─┐
│                              │
│     I think (that) . . .     │
│     In my opinion, . . .     │
│     I'd like to say (that) . . . │
│     May I say (that) . . . ?  │
│     Can I answer that?       │
│     Can I respond to that?   │
│                              │
└──────────────────────────────┘
```

Format: Small Groups – A, p. 32; B, p. 98; C, p. 156; D, p. 157

Directions for Asking

(1) Ask your questions below in any order.

(2) ***Do not ask anyone directly.*** (In other words, don't look at anyone or say anyone's name.)

(3) Your partners will volunteer to answer.

Directions for Volunteering

(1) ***Volunteer to answer*** your partners' questions ***with details.*** (Answer with **and, but, so, because,** or **two sentences.**)

(2) Try to answer first sometimes, and sometimes wait for your partners to volunteer.

(3) Ask follow-up questions, too.

Questions for volunteers to answer

- What actor or actress would you like to meet?
- Would you marry a foreigner?
- Are you a "morning person" or a "night person"?
- What did you buy the last time you went shopping?
- In your family, who knows the most about computers?
- (You think of some questions.)

E
E
E
E
E
E

Volunteering an Answer

Discussion

Format: Triads – Student A, page 33; Student B, page 99
Topic: Divorce

Part 1

Pre-discussion
(1) Before starting this discussion of divorce in Europe, ask
   your partners these questions.
(2) Answer their questions.

3. Which of these countries do you think has the highest divorce
   rate? (a) Britain (b) Sweden (c) Spain   (d) Greece
6. In general, what do you think is the most common reason for
   divorce?
   a) The couple doesn't have similar interests.
   b) Violence, i.e., the husband or wife hits or beats the other
      one.
   c) Poor communication, in other words, the spouses don't talk
      to each other much or they often have disagreements.
   d) The husband or wife has a secret lover.

Part 2

Discussion Directions
(1) Listen to Student A read the first part of the article.
(2) Listen to Student B read the second part of the article.
(3) Read your third part of the article to your partners.

DIVORCE (C)

It's interesting to see why the divorce rate is lower in
some European countries than in others. In Italy, there
are few divorces, probably because Italians believe marriages
should continue forever. Furthermore, in general, Italian

This news story continues on page 161.

C
C
C
C
C
C

HEY! WHERE'S THE CANDLES?.. WE USED TO HAVE CANDLES EVERY NIGHT ... are you listening to me?

Many Young People feel it is important to have a Romantic Relationship....... They expect to have a perfect marriage

women cannot make as much money as men, so they need men's financial support. Finally, in Italy having a lover outside of marriage is widely acceptable. In other words, most Italians would not want a divorce if they found out that their spouse had a secret lover.

Another country with a low divorce rate is Spain. Actually, divorce was illegal in Spain until 1981. Also, like Italian women, Spanish women need men's financial support. But the most important reason why the divorce rate is low in Spain is that the extended family is very important there. In an extended family, children, parents, grandparents and even great-grandparents live together. Spanish men feel it is their responsibility to stay with their families and take care of their children.

Finally, what are the reasons people get divorced? The most common reason is violence, when one of the spouses hits or beats the other one. Some other reasons are (1) the couple is unable to communicate with each other, (2) a spouse has a secret lover, (3) a spouse has a problem with alcohol or drugs, and (4) the couple has no common interest.

Part 3

Factual Questions about the news story

Read the questions in Part 1 to your partners again and try to answer their questions.

Part 4

Reaction Questions about your partners' opinions

Your Feelings about Marriage and Divorce

3. What do you think is a good age to get married?
6. When you were a child, did you live with an extended family? Do you think it was good that your grandparents did or didn't live with you?
9. Is it common for women in your country to have children outside of marriage?

Discussion   • *161*

C
C
C
C
C
C

Clarifying by Summarizing, II

Focus: Summarizing (clarifications are not provided)
Format: Triads – Student A, page 40; Student B, page 105
Topic: Catching Colds

Before Part 1 of the discussion
   (1) *Silently* read this last part of the article (C) in Part 3.
   (2) Write answers to the *Factual Questions* in Part 4.

Parts 1 & 2
   (1) Listen to your partners read the first two parts of the article.
   (2) Ask **summary clarification questions** when asked if
       you understand, *even if you do understand clearly.*
   (3) Use the following expressions.

Summary Clarification Questions

Did you say _____ ?   You mean _____ ?

You said _____, right?   In other words, _____, right?

I think you said _____, right?

I'm not sure I understand. Did you say _____ ?

Part 3
   (1) Read this last part of the article to your partners.
   (2) Answer their **summary clarification questions**.

Catching Colds (C)

How do we know when we're catching a cold? Usually, a cold
starts in our throat; we start to feel a sore throat. Then the cold
moves to our nose, and we start to have a runny nose. Our
bodies will start to fight the cold and, after about a week, our
bodies will win the fight and we will feel healthy again. **Have
you got this first paragraph?**

This news story is continued on the next page.

C
C
C
C
C
C

                 Clarifying by Summarizing, II

If our cold continues for more than two weeks, it probably means we don't really have a cold at all. Instead, we may have something more serious. In that case, we should go to a doctor. **Understand?**

The average adult gets two or three colds every year. On the other hand, children and teenagers get five to ten colds a year. This is because adults have developed a defense system against the types of colds they had when they were younger. But children need to catch a cold first in order to build a defense. Also, children catch more colds because they don't wash their hands often and because often they put their hands in their mouths after touching something dirty. **Got it?**

Part 4

Factual Questions about the article
Ask these questions and answer your partners'.

3. Where do we first feel a cold in our bodies?

6. If you have a cold for more than two weeks, what should you do? Why?

9. Who gets more colds every year, adults or children? Why?

Reaction Questions about your partners' opinions and experiences. Ask these questions and ask follow-up questions.

You and the Common Cold

3. When you were younger, did you ever miss several days of school because you were sick?
6. What health problem have you had recently?
9. Do you think your hometown is a healthy place to live?

C
C
C
C
C
C

Clarifying by Summarizing, II   • *163*

Telling Other People's Opinions and Experiences

Format: Small Groups – A, page 42; B, page 107; D, page 166

Part 1
(1) Discuss the *topics* below with your partners.
(2) Try to give details and ask questions to get more details.
(3) Listen closely to what your partners say, because in Part 2 you will tell new groups what they said.

Discussion topics
3. Tell us what you were doing last year at this time.
7. Tell us about the job you would like to have in the future.

Expressions for Telling Others' Opinions and Experiences

I have no opinion about that,
    but I know someone who . . .
I haven't, but _____ **has.**
          (friend's name)

I've never done that, but my friend . . .
I'm not sure, but someone told me . . .
I don't know, but I do know someone who . . .

Part 2
(1) Get into new groups.
(2) Ask your new partners the questions below. Answer their questions by telling what you learned in your first group in Part 1. Use the expressions for "Telling Others' Opinions and Experiences."
(3) ***Do not tell your own opinions or experiences***.
(4) Ask questions to get more details.

Unit 20 continues on the next page.

Discussion questions

3. What were you doing last year at this time?
7. What job would you like to have in the future?

Part 3

(1) Discuss the *topics* below with your partners.
(2) Try to give details and ask questions to get more details.
(3) Listen closely to what your partners say, because in Part 4 you will form a new group and tell what they said.

More discussion topics

3. Tell us about a movie you've seen recently.
7. Tell us the name of a famous person you would like to be.

Part 4

Directions

(1) Get into new groups again.
(2) Ask your new partners the questions below. Answer their questions by telling what you learned in your second group in Part 3. Use the expressions for "Telling Others' Opinions and Experiences."
(3) ***Do not give your own opinions or experiences***.
(4) Ask questions to get more details.

More discussion questions

3. Have you seen any movies recently?
7. What famous person would you like to be?

Telling Other People's Opinions and Experiences

Format: Small Groups – A, page 42; B, page 107; C, page 164

Part 1
(1) Discuss the *topics* below with your partners.
(2) Try to give details and ask questions to get more details.
(3) Listen closely to what your partners say, because in Part 2 you will tell new groups what they said.

Discussion topics
4. Tell us about one of your recent problems.
8. Tell us about a famous person you've met.

Expressions for Re-telling Others' Opinions and Experiences

I have no opinion about that,
    but I know someone who . . .
I haven't, but _____ has.
                    (friend's name)

I've never done that, but my friend . . .
I'm not sure, but someone told me . . .
I don't know, but I do know someone who . . .

Part 2
(1) Get into new groups.
(2) Ask your new partners the questions below. Answer their questions by telling what you learned in your first group in Part 1. Use the expressions for "Telling Others' Opinions and Experiences."
(3) ***Do not tell your own opinions or experiences***.
(4) Ask questions to get more details.

Unit 20 continues on the next page.

D
D
D
D
D
D

Discussion questions
4. What problem have you had recently?
8. What famous person have you met?

Part 3
(1) Discuss the *topics* below with your partners.
(2) Try to give details and ask questions to get more details.
(3) Listen closely to what your partners say, because in Part 4 you will form a new group and tell what they said.

More discussion topics
4. Tell us about a time when you were punished by your teacher or parents.
8. Tell us about an insect or animal that you're afraid of or that disgusts you.

Part 4

Directions
(1) Get into new groups again.
(2) Ask your new partners the questions below. Answer their questions by telling what you learned in your second group in Part 3. Use the expressions for "Telling Others' Opinions and Experiences."
(3) ***Do not give your own opinions or experiences***.
(4) Ask questions to get more details.

More discussion questions
4. Were you ever punished by your teacher or parents?
8. Are you afraid of any animals or insects?

D
D
D
D
D

Discussion

Format: **Triads** – Student A, page 44; Student B, page 109
Topic: Driving

Before Part 1 of the discussion
(1) *Silently* read your article about driving in Part 3.
(2) Write answers to your *Factual Questions* and write two
    more questions.
(3) Write two more *Reaction Questions* in Part 4.

Parts 1 & 2
(1) Listen to your partners read the first and second articles.
(2) Interrupt to ask them clarification questions when you don't
    understand.
(3) Answer their *Factual Questions*.

Part 3
(1) Read this last article to your partners.
(2) Then ask your *Factual Questions*.

Driving a Stolen Car

Mike Morris wanted to go to the grocery store, but he
couldn't use his car because his mother's blue van was
parked behind his in the driveway. So he borrowed his
mother's van and drove to a shopping center. After buying
some groceries and putting them in the van, he decided
to shop in a couple of other stores at the shopping
center. When he returned to the blue van, he noticed that
his bags of groceries were gone, so he thought someone
had broken into the van and stolen them. As he was

This story continues on the next page.

C
C
C
C
C

Discussion

driving back home, he suddenly heard some police sirens and noticed flashing lights behind him. He stopped his van, got out, and saw five policemen with their guns pointed at him. Then he realized his mistake; he had taken the wrong blue van. Surprisingly, the key to his mother's van also worked in the other van, too! After returning to the shopping center with Mike and seeing his mother's van, the police believed his story and let him go.

Factual Questions about your article
Ask your partners these questions.

1. Why didn't Mike drive his car to the shopping center?

   _____

2. What did he do after he bought some groceries?

   _____

3. _____

4. _____

Part 4

Reaction Questions about your partners' opinions and experiences
Ask these reaction questions and some follow-up questions. Write two more questions to ask. Answer your partners' questions with details.

Stolen Cars

9. In your country, is it necessary to lock your car doors whenever you leave your car in a parking lot?

10. Have you ever been in a car that was stopped by the police?

11. _____

12. _____

C
C
C
C
C
C

Discussion

Helping the Discussion Leader Explain, I

Format: Triads – Student A, page 47; Student B, page 112

Expressions

Could you help me explain that?
Do you know what I mean?

Example

A: When I got up this morning, I felt irritable.
B: What do you mean by "irritable"?
A (to Student C): Could you help me explain that?
C (to Student B): Sure. He means he was in a
bad mood. He was cross, grumpy, and mad at the
world when he got up this morning.

Part 1
(1) Student A will read some sentences to Student B.
(2) Student B will ask Student A clarification questions.
(3) Student A will ask you to help clarify for Student B. Help
Student A explain. Try to have a brief discussion about the
topic of each sentence.

Unit 22 continues on the next page.

C
C
C
C
C
C

Part 2

   (1) Student B will read some sentences to you.
   (2) You ask Student B the five clarification questions below.
   (3) Student B will ask Student A to help clarify the sentences for you.

    1. (Student B) , I'm afraid I don't know what "athlete" means.

    2. Can you give me an example of a pet?

    3. I'm not sure I understand the word "stress." Can you give me some examples of what happens to a person who's feeling stress?

    4. I'm not sure I understand the question.

    5. What do you mean by the word "homesick"?

Part 3

   (1) Read the following sentences to Student A.
   (2) Student A will ask you to clarify, but **you don't clarify.**
   (3) Ask Student B to help you explain the sentences. Try to have a brief discussion about the topic of each of these sentences.

    1. (Student A) , is there much crime in your hometown?
       After Student C's clarification question:
       (Student B) , could you help me explain?

    2. When I was a child and did something naughty, my parents spanked me.

    3. What were some things you worried about when you were a pre-teen?

    4. Did you belong to any clubs when you were in high school?

    5. When I was younger, I often got poor grades because I had bad study habits.

C
C
C
C
C
C

Helping the Discussion Leader Explain, I

∽ Unit 23 • Student C
Helping the Discussion
Leader Explain, II

Format: **Triads** – Student A, page 49; Student B, page 114
Topic: Part 1. Fathers Who Live Longer
          Part 2. Smoking and Aging
          Part 3. Tasting Foods

Before Part 1 of the discussion
 (1) *Silently* read your article about tasting food in Part 3.
 (2) Write answers to your *Factual Questions* and write two
     more questions.
 (3) Write two more *Reaction Questions* in Part 4.

Parts 1 & 2
 (1) Listen to your partners read their articles.
 (2) For practice, ask **clarification questions**, *even if you*
     understand clearly.

Part 3
 (1) Read this article to your partners.
 (2) Don't answer your partners' clarification questions.
 (3) Ask a partner to help you explain.
 (4) Try to use the **"Help the Leader" Expressions.**
 (5) Ask your *Factual Questions*.

"Help the Leader"
Expressions

Could you help me explain that?
Do you know what I mean?

Unit 23 continues on the next page.

Helping the Discussion Leader Explain, II   **• 173**

C
C
C
C
C

Tasting Food

Scientists have been studying the reasons why some people don't like the taste of certain vegetables. They found that people inherit some genes from their parents that cause them to like or dislike certain tastes. **Did you understand?**

In their research about tastes, scientists found that there are three types of people in the world. First, there are "nontasters," who are not very sensitive to sweet-tasting foods or bitter-tasting foods. The people of the second type are just called "tasters," and those of the third are "supertasters," who are very sensitive to sweet and bitter flavors. Children of the third type, who are supertasters, will probably not like vegetables such as broccoli and brussel sprouts because of their bitter taste. This is unfortunate, because supertasters might avoid eating foods that are important for their health. **OK?**

The scientists said that thousands of years ago, on the other hand, supertasters actually had an advantage over other types of people. At that time, supertasters could avoid eating bitter-tasting poisonous plants which other types of people would eat. **Got it?**

From this research about tastes, we learn some interesting things about supertasters. For one thing, supertasters have more taste buds on their tongues. And, to super-tasters, bitter foods taste *very* bitter, and sweet foods taste *very* sweet. Supertasters might also not like spicy food made with chili pepper, because it would be too hot for them. Furthermore, female supertasters probably won't be very fat, but they do seem to enjoy cooking more than other types of people. **Understand?**

Factual Questions about the article

Ask these questions about the article.

1. _____

2. What are the three types of people in the world?

   _____

3. Is this statement true or false? Thousands of years ago, supertasters probably ate many poisonous plants.

   _____

4. _____

Part 4

Reaction Questions about your partners' opinions and experiences

1. About the article on tasting food, do you think you're a supertaster?

2. In general, do you prefer the food from your own country or from other countries?

3. _____

4. _____

C
C
C
C
C
C

Discussion

Format: Triads – Student A, page 52; Student B, page 117
Topic: Gambling

Before Part 1 of the discussion
    (1) *Silently* read your part of the article about gambling in Part 3.
    (2) Write answers to your *Factual Questions* and write two
        more questions.

Parts 1 & 2
    (1) Listen to your partners read the first two parts of the article.
    (2) Interrupt to ask them clarification questions when you don't
        understand.
    (3) Answer their *Factual Questions*.

Part 3
    (1) Read this last part of the article to your partners.
    (2) Then ask them your *Factual Questions*.

Gambling (C)

Here is a story about a woman who became a compulsive gambler. Her name is Rose. She was a wife and mother who lived in a comfortable suburb of New York. Rose had never gambled in her life because it was illegal — until New York State started a lottery. Then she bought some lottery tickets.

After a few weeks, Rose won some money. She felt confident that she would soon become a millionaire. So she started to play other lottery games, too, and started spending $100 and then $300 a week. Soon she had spent all the money in her family's bank account and started using her credit cards to borrow more money for gambling.

This article continues on the next page.

Her family didn't know about her gambling problems. After her husband got sick and died, she started gambling even more. Soon she owed more than $100,000. In the end, she was able to stop gambling only after joining an organization that helps compulsive gamblers control their habit.

Factual Questions about your article
Ask your partners these questions.

1. _____

2. What was the first thing Rose gambled on?

_____

3. Why didn't she quit gambling after she lost money?

_____

4. _____

Part 4

Reaction Questions about your partners' opinions and experiences. Ask the questions below and some follow-up questions. Answer your partners' questions with details.

Lady Luck and You

3. Do you know anyone who is compulsive (for example, a compulsive shopper, eater, worker, or computer-game player)?

6. Have you ever borrowed money for anything?

(Think of two more *Reaction Questions* about gambling.)

C
C
C
C
C
C

Expressing Opinions, II

Format: Small Groups – A, page 58; B, page 123; D, page 182
Topics: Part 1. The Rights of Mothers and Fathers
Part 2. Death Caused by Cigarettes
Part 3. De-barking Dogs
Part 4. 63-year-old Woman Has a Baby

Agreeing

That's a good point.
I totally agree with _____.
That's right.

Disagreeing

I'm afraid I disagree.
That's a good point, but . . .
Actually, I think . . .

Before Part 1 of the discussion
Silently read this article about a way to stop dogs from barking in Part 3.

Parts 1 & 2
(1) Listen to Students A & B read the first and second articles.
(2) Answer and discuss their questions.

Part 3
(1) Read your article to your partners.
(2) Then ask the *Factual* and *Reaction Questions*.

Unit 26 is continued on the next page.

C
C
C
C
C
C

De-barking Dogs

Mike lives in an apartment with his dog, Candy. When Mike leaves home, Candy barks. She barks at the mailman, at the door bell, and at the neighbor's dog. The owner of Mike's apartment told him that Candy has to stop barking, or Mike will have to move out of his apartment. He doesn't want to move, and he doesn't want to find a new owner for Candy, so Mike asked two animal doctors for advice. The first doctor suggested that they operate on Candy in order to cut the vocal cords. Then, Candy would not be able to bark. This is called "de-barking." This first doctor also said that it is easy to do, and dogs recover quickly. It doesn't cause any health problems, and it doesn't change their personality. Also, after the operation, the dogs seem normal and happy. They can still make a noise, but the sound is very soft. Mike talked to a second animal doctor. He said that de-barking a dog can cause problems. It can cause some difficulty when dogs breathe. Also, he said that the reason why dogs bark is because they are bored. They need to do something and to stay busy! In order to control Candy's barking, this second doctor recommended that Mike put a special collar around Candy's neck. Then, when she barks, the collar will spray a bad smell in her face. By doing that, Mike could avoid the de-barking operation.

C
C
C
C
C
C

Factual Questions about the article
Ask these questions about the article.

1. The first doctor recommended de-barking Candy. What were the reasons?
2. The second doctor was against the idea of de-barking. What were the reasons?

Reaction Questions about your partners' opinions. Ask these questions about the article. Agree or disagree with your partners. Express your own opinions as well.

Stopping a Dog from Barking

1. If your neighbor had a dog that barked all the time, and you couldn't sleep at night, what advice would you give your neighbor?
2. If you lived in an apartment that you loved, and your neighbors said that your dog barked too much, what would you do?

Part 4

(1) Listen to Student D read the last article.
(2) Answer and discuss their questions.

Expressing Opinions, II

C
C
C
C
C

Student D • Unit 26 ⌒

Expressing Opinions, II

Format: **Small Groups** – A, page 58; B, page 123; C, page 179
Topics: Part 1.   The Rights of Mothers and Fathers
Part 2.   Death Caused by Cigarettes
Part 3.   De-barking Dogs
Part 4.   63-year-old Woman Has a Baby

Agreeing

That's a good point.

I totally agree with _____.

That's right.

Disagreeing

I'm afraid I disagree.

That's a good point, but . . .

Actually, I think . . .

Before Part 1 of the discussion
Silently read this article about the 63-year-old woman having a baby in Part 4.

Parts 1, 2, & 3
(1)   Listen to Students A, B, & C read their articles.
(2)   Answer and discuss their questions.

Part 4
(1)   Read your article to your partners.
(2)   Then ask the *Factual* and *Reaction Questions*.

Unit 26 is continued on the next page.

Expressing Opinions, II

63-year-old Woman Has a Baby

Recently, a woman who was 63 years old had a baby. Even though she was past the age when a woman can get pregnant naturally, she was able to do it through a laboratory. Some people think that a woman at this age shouldn't have a baby; others think she has a right to.

The woman said she wanted to have a baby because she had never had any children, and she wanted to experience childbirth. Besides, she wanted someone to continue her family's name. People who agree with her decision say that she will be a better mother than many younger mothers because she is mature and has a lot of life experiences. They also say she has more time to spend with her child than many younger mothers, who are busy with their careers and other activities; moreover, she has more money to spend on her child than many young mothers do. Finally, they say few people become upset when men in their 60s became fathers, so it's only fair that women should also be able to.

People who oppose her decision to have a baby say it's unnatural for women at this age to have babies. They say a woman in her 60s shouldn't need to get pregnant in order to feel valuable. These people also say that it's not fair to the child. When the child is 15, her mother will be 78. This teenage child will have the responsibility that many people in their 40s and 50s have of taking care of older relatives. It will be like a teenager taking care of her grandparents.

D
D
D
D
D

Factual Questions about the article

Ask these questions about the article.

1. Why did this woman decide to have a baby?
2. Why do some people disagree with her decision?

Reaction Questions about your partners' opinions. Ask these questions about the article. Agree or disagree with your partners. Express your own opinions as well.

Too Old for Motherhood?

1. Do you think that it was a good idea for this woman to have a baby?
2. Should there be a law against older women having babies?

Expressing Opinions, II

Referring to a Source

Format: Triads – Student A, page 61; Student B, page 126
Topic: Bullying

```
┌─── Referring to a Source ───┐
│                             │
│   I read that _____.   │
│   I heard that _____.  │
│   According to an article I read, _____. │
│   According to the newspaper, _____.   │
│                             │
└─────────────────────────────┘
```

Before Part 1 of the discussion
- (1) *Silently* read the information from the article about bullying.
- (2) **Do not read this article to your partners.**

Bullying (C)

This article about bullying explains what can be done to help children who are victims of bullying, and what the victims themselves can do to stop the bullies.

There are several things parents can do if their child is a victim of bullying. One thing is to practice with the child what to say or do when the bully tries to hurt them. In other words, the parents and child can role play; the kid plays the part of the bully, and the parent plays the part of the victim. Also, parents can help children make friends by encouraging them to invite classmates to their home or by encouraging the children to join clubs. Parents can also help siblings to get along. Kids who have close relationships with friends and siblings will have a feeling of support when confronted by a bully.

Some cities that have bullying problems have 24-hour hot lines that victims can call if they need help and advice.

This article is continued on the next page.

C
C
C
C
C
C

Referring to a Source

There are also some things victims can do to discourage
bullies. First, the victim shouldn't react by crying. A bully
is trying to get a reaction, so if the victim can remain
calm, then the bully won't be rewarded. Second, the victim
can respond but not fight back. They can say to the bully,
"Don't do that. I'll report you." The victim can also try to
explain to the bully how they feel; however, it's a good idea
to do this when the bully is alone instead of when they're
with their friends. Finally, it's a good idea for the victim to
have friends around when the bully is near.
Source: *The Observer*

Parts 1 & 2

Answer your partners' questions by giving your opinion.
You don't have to refer to a source.

Part 3

(1) Don't read this article to your partners.
(2) Instead, ask the following questions.
(3) After your partners answer, tell them what you
    have learned from the article. Don't read it to them.
(4) Try to use the expressions for **"Referring to a Source."**

Questions for your partners

1. What do you think parents can do to help a child who is the
   victim of a bully?
2. What do you think kids should do if they're victims of bullying?

Part 4

**Discussion about your partners' opinions and experiences
with bullying.** Ask your partners these questions, and answer
their questions.

3. When you were younger, did you ever have a fight with anyone?
6. In school, did you ever help another student who was a victim
   of bullying?

C
C
C
C
C
C

186 •

Summary Discussion

Format: Triads – Student A, page 64; Student B, page 129

Topics: Part 1. Best Friends
           Part 2. The Effects of Watching TV
           Part 3. Spanking

Before Part 1

(1) Review the Discussion Strategies with your partner(s).
(2) First, fill in the blanks in the Summary box below by asking each other for examples.
(3) Then go back to the unit where the strategy is introduced to review other phrases and expressions.
(4) Then *silently* read your article in Part 1.

— Discussion Strategies Summary —

Rejoinders (Unit 1)	_____
Follow-up Questions (Unit 1)	_____
Clarification Expressions (Unit 2)	*Did you say that . . . ?*
Comprehension Checks (Unit 3)	_____
Answering with Details (Unit 5)	_____
Interrupting (Unit 12)	*Could I ask something?*
Words That Describe (Unit 13)	_____
Re-telling Something (Unit 15)	_____
Volunteering an Answer (Unit 16)	*May/Can I answer that?*
Summary Clarification Questions (Unit 19)	_____
Re-telling Others' Opinions (Unit 20)	_____
Helping the Leader (Unit 22)	*Could you help me explain that?*
Expressing Opinions (Unit 25)	_____
Referring to a Source (Unit 27)	_____

Summary Discussion

C
C
C
C
C
C

Summary Discussion

Parts 1 & 2
  (1) Listen to your partners read their articles.
  (2) Then discuss their articles with them, using discussion
         strategies.

Part 3
  (1) Read this article to your partners.
  (2) Then discuss it, using the strategies above.

Spanking

This article talks about spanking children. Researchers
have discovered that problems are caused when parents
spank their children. They found that hitting children
actually makes them behave even worse than before.
In other words, spanking children increases aggressive
behavior.

Parents often think that by using corporal punishment,
they will make their children behave better. This may be
true at first, but a month or even a year later, these kids
show antisocial behavior. Some examples of antisocial
behavior are lying, cheating, bullying, breaking things on
purpose, disobeying teachers, and not apologizing.

Researchers compared the behavior of children who had
and hadn't been spanked. Over a two-year period, they
interviewed 800 mothers of children between the ages of
six and nine. The week before the interview, 44% of the

This article continues on the next page.

C
C
C
C
C
C

mothers had spanked their children an average of twice
during that week. The results showed that the more
children were spanked, the more they behaved in an
antisocial manner. Many people think that if parents
hit their children "because they love them," there will
be no harmful effect. However, research shows that this
is not true.

Part 4

Discuss your discussion

(1) Did you use a lot of the strategies you've been practicing?
(2) Which ones did you use?
    Which ones didn't you use? Why not?

A Teacher-led Discussion

Format: Whole-class or **large-group**
Topic: Working Mothers

For Teachers Only
Possible formats:
(1) The teacher models as a leader of a whole-class discussion.
(2) In a class with strong discussion skills, one or two students serve as a leaders of a whole-class discussion.
(3) With a large and strong class divided, several students serve as leaders of large-group discussions.

Procedure
(1) The **leader(s)** silently reads the article about working mothers and writes several *Factual and Reaction Questions*.
(2) The **leader** reads the article and leads a discussion by asking the questions. The **members** should be encouraged to interrupt and use discussion strategies such as asking clarification questions, volunteering to answer, answering with details, helping the leader, and so on.

Cheating in School

Why is cheating in school so common? A survey found that 90% of college students said that cheating is wrong. However, 90% of them said that they had cheated at some time in the past.

The survey found that, not surprisingly, most college students cheat because they feel pressure to get good grades. The survey also found some other interesting facts. Men were more likely to cheat than women. Also, students at large universities cheat more than students at smaller colleges.

This article is continued on the next page.

A Model Teacher-led Discussion • 191

Interestingly, very young children rarely cheat. Perhaps the reason for this is that in order to cheat, a child needs to have basic reading and writing skills, and most young children don't have these skills. In addition, when young children do cheat, they often do not understand that it is wrong to do it. They mainly do it because they see that it is an easy way to get a reward that comes with getting a good grade.

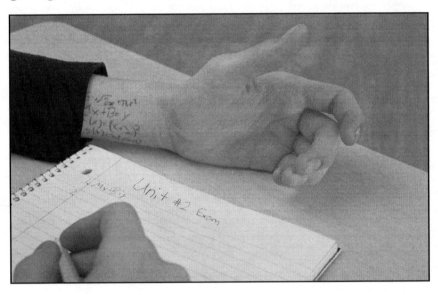

During high school years, the rate of cheating increases greatly. These students see cheating as an easy solution to a difficult challenge. The challenge is how to meet the expectations of their parents and teachers.

Many parents don't know what do if they find out that their son or daughter has been cheating. Most parents think that cheating is more serious than other serious

This article is continued on the next page.

problems, like fighting. The reason for this might be be-cause if a child is fighting, he will probably have physical signs on his body, for example, torn clothes or an injury. However, if a child is cheating, parents probably won't know about it unless a teacher tells them.

One reason why children cheat is because they see situations in which their parents cheat. For example, if they go to a movie theater with their parents, the parents might try to pay "children prices" for a movie ticket, even though their child is a teenager. Another example could happen at a store. If the parents pay for something and the clerk accidentally gives back too much change, the parents might not tell the clerk about the mistake. These situations show how parents can be bad examples. And from these examples, children might learn that if they want to get a good grade, it is okay to use any technique, even cheating.

What should parents do if they find out that their child is cheating? To begin with, they should not get angry and punish the child. This will put more pressure on the child and perhaps cause him to cheat even more. Instead, par-ents should do two things. First, they should explain to the child why cheating is wrong. And second, they should help the child develop good study skills so that he can pass the next test honestly.

Instructions for Leading a Discussion

Format: Groups

Preparation Steps
  (1) Get in groups of 2, 3, or 4 students.
  (2) With your partners, choose one of the discussion topics
       listed on the next page, and tell your teacher your choice.
       Each group must choose a different topic, and each of
       you will lead a discussion on this topic.
  (3) Go to the page with the reading you have chosen for your
       discussion and read the article. Help each other understand
       all the words. ***Don't read the other articles.***
  (4) With your partners, write five *Factual Questions* about the
       article and eight to ten additional *Reaction Questions*.
  (5) Practice reading the article.
  (6) Your teacher will provide a schedule of when you'll serve as
       a group leader and when you'll be a discussion participant.

When you're the discussion group leader
  You'll be a discussion group leader for about 40 minutes.
  (Each of your partners will be the leader of another group.)
  (1) Read your article to your group and use lots of **discussion
       strategies** (e.g., ask them if they understand, answer their
       clarification questions and ask members to help you explain,
       explain words they don't understand, and ask members
       to help you explain).
  (2) Ask the five *Factual Questions* you have written.
  (3) Ask your *Reaction Questions*, and use **discussion strategies**
       (e.g., ask follow-up questions, ask for more details).

When you're a member of a discussion group
  (1) Each discussion will be led by one person. Everyone else will
       participate as discussion group members.
  (2) Try to be an active member by using **discussion strategies**
       (e.g., ask clarification questions, answer with details, ask
       other members follow-up questions, volunteer answers,
       clarify by summarizing, and help the leader explain).

Units 30-38 • For Students, continued

Choose one of these articles:

Unit 30   *Animal Empathy*
Research finds that animals understand the feelings of others.

Unit 31   *Cafeteria Trays*
Studies find that using trays encourages students to waste
food in cafeterias.

Unit 32   *TV in the Bedroom*
This article explains the bad effects having a TV in their
bedroom has on children.

Unit 33   *Culture and Alcoholism*
People from several different countries talk about how alcohol
and alcohol abuse are viewed in their countries.

Unit 34   *Boredom*
Studies show the relation between technology and boredom
and that boredom has a negative impact on individuals and
society.

Unit 35   *Keys to Happiness*
This article explains several factors in people's lives that make
them happy.

Unit 36   *The Clown and the Cell Phones*
Research demonstrates that people using cell phones are
generally unaware of their surroundings

Unit 37   *Family Meals*
This article explores several ways in which is good for families
to eat together. It is good for them physically, psychologically,
and socially.

Unit 38   *International Students in the U.S.*
Two international students tell about their experiences in a
North American school.

Instructions for Leading a Discussion   **• 195**

Format: Large Group/Whole Class

Animal Empathy

This article is about empathy. "Empathy" means that you can understand the feelings of other people. Some people believe that animals can feel empathy too. In other words, they think that animals can understand how people or other animals feel.

One example of this situation happened in Russia. A woman in Russia had a pet monkey. Sometimes, the monkey climbed up on the roof of her house and wouldn't come down, even if she called it. So the woman put a plate of food on the ground for the monkey. But it still refused to come down. So, the woman sat on the ground and pretended that she was hurt. She also started crying in a loud voice. Soon, the monkey came down from the roof, sat next to the woman, and put its arm around her! This seemed to show that the monkey felt empathy.

Here is another example of animal empathy. There was a chimpanzee named Kuni, who lived in a zoo. She lived outside in an area that was surrounded by a glass fence. People could watch her through the glass fence. One day, a bird flew into her area, hit the glass fence and fell on the ground. The bird couldn't move. So Kuni carefully picked up the bird and climbed a tree. Then, she spread the bird's wings with her fingers and gently threw it up into the air. She was trying to help the bird fly! This seemed to show that Kuni understood what the bird needed. Unfortunately, the bird just fell to the ground. Kuni sat next to the bird and seemed to protect it. After a few hours, the bird recovered and flew away.

Unit 30 is continued on the next page.

Researchers did another experiment with monkeys in a laboratory. There were two groups of monkeys. One group was called "actors," and the other group was called "receivers." Each "actor" monkey was put in a cage with two chains. When he saw a light turn on, he could pull one of the chains, and he would get some food. Then, the researchers changed the experiment in this way. Next to the "actor" monkey's cage, they put another cage, with a "receiver" monkey. Also, they added colored lights. If a blue light turned on, and the "actor" monkey pulled one of the chains, he could get food, and if a red light turned on, he could get food if he pulled the other chain. However, if the red light turned on and he pulled the chain to get food, the "receiver" monkey in the next cage would receive a strong electric shock. The "receiver" monkey would often scream when he got the shock. It is interesting that two of the 15 "actor" monkeys completely stopped pulling the chain when the red light came on. In other words, they stopped pulling the chain that gave them food and gave the other monkey a shock. This meant that they completely stopped eating. Also, if the "receiver" monkey was a family member, they were even less likely to pull the chain that gave a shock. As a result, it seems that these monkeys were feeling empathy.

Factual Questions about the article

1. _____
2. _____
3. _____
4. _____
5. _____

Reaction Questions about your opinions and experiences
(You can write your own questions and/or choose some of these.)

- This article told about the chimpanzee who climbed to the roof of his house, about the chimpanzee and the bird, and about the monkeys that gave electric shocks.Were you surprised by any of these stories?
- Have you ever had a pet that you think could feel empathy?
- Researchers often use monkeys for medical research. For example, they use them to try to find cures for diseases like cancer. Sometimes these monkeys die as a result of the experiments. Do you think that it's okay to do this if it means that it could save people's lives?

Format: Large Group/Whole Class

Cafeteria Trays

Some American colleges are finding ways to save money and at the same time, save the environment. At American colleges, many students eat their meals in a cafeteria. Often, they will pay one price for the month, and then they can eat as much food as they want.

When students enter a cafeteria, the first thing they do is to pick up a large plastic tray. Then they walk along a counter, take the plates of food and glasses of drinks that they want, and put them on the tray. After they have done this, they carry the tray to a table and begin to eat. Because students are often very hungry when they come into the cafeteria, they sometimes take more food than they can really eat. Unfortunately, the food that they don't eat is thrown into the garbage. One student who had a major in environmental studies did some research. She asked all the students in one cafeteria to put their leftovers into large plastic bins. ("Leftovers" are food that you don't completely eat during a meal.) In two days, they had about 400 pounds of food that students were throwing away. That is about 181 kilograms.

Now, some college cafeterias have stopped using trays. And they have found some positive results. First, there has been a big drop in wasted food. In fact, one college cafeteria saved 10 percent of the money that it spent on food. There is a reason for this. When students don't have a tray, they can carry only one or two plates in their hands. They take

Unit 31 is continued on the next page.

Nine Discussion Choices

those to their table. After eating that food, they have time to decide if they really want more food or not. If they do, they must stand in line again to get it. Many students don't want to do this unless they are really hungry.

Another advantage is saving water. At one college cafeteria, they washed 147,000 (that is, one hundred-forty-seven thousand) trays in one year. And they used 14,000 gallons of water to wash them. That's 53,000 liters. When they stopped using trays, they were able to save all that water!

A final positive result is about students' weight. Often, when students leave home and go to college, they don't eat the right kind of food or the proper amount of food. In the cafeterias, they can eat as much food as they want, so students often eat too much, especially things like cake and ice cream. As a result, they become overweight. After the trays were taken out of the cafeteria, one student said that she lost 10 pounds (four and half kilograms).

Factual Questions about the article

1. _____
2. _____
3. _____
4. _____
5. _____

Reaction Questions about your opinions and experiences
(You can write your own questions and/or choose some of these.)

• In your country, do college students eat in cafeterias? If they do, do they use trays?
• Is there a problem with students becoming overweight in your country?
• What things do you do to help the environment?
• Does your country have any special environmental problems?

Format: Large Group/Whole Class

TV in the Bedroom

About half of American children have a TV in their bedrooms. Now, researchers are finding that this situation might cause some health problems for these children.

Children who have TVs in the bedroom get lower scores on school tests, and they are more likely to have sleeping problems. Also, there is a big chance that these kids will be overweight and become smokers.

In a study of 80 children who were between the ages of four and seven years old, researchers found that children who did not have a TV in the bedroom watched 21 hours of TV a week. But children who had a TV in the bedroom watched nine hours more a week— in other words, 30 hours a week total! They also found that the parents did not realize that the children were watching so many hours of TV. In addition, the parents didn't even know what types of programs their kids were watching!

In one interesting experiment, researchers put a device (or tool) on all the TVs in a house. The device turned off the TV after a period of

Unit 32 is continued on the next page.

Nine Discussion Choices

time. For example, after an hour, the TV turned off. If the children wanted to watch more TV, they had to use a code in order to turn the TV on again. This is what they found from the experiment. The kids lost weight if they lived in a house that had the device. However, surprisingly, they did not exercise more than the other kids. Instead, they just ate less junk food. This result seems to show that TV and eating junk food are connected in some way.

A study in France also found that kids who had a TV in the bedroom were more likely to be overweight. And, not surprisingly, these kids spent less time reading than other kids.

In another study, in California, researchers looked at children who had a TV or computer in the bedroom. The children who had a TV had much lower grades in reading and math than children who did not have their own TV. In contrast, children who had a computer had higher grades.

These studies show that watching too much TV can be harmful for children.

Factual Questions about the article

1. _____
2. _____
3. _____
4. _____
5. _____

Reaction Questions about your opinions and experiences
(You can write your own questions and/or choose some of these.)

• Is it common for children to have a TV in the bedroom in your country?
• Did you often watch TV alone when you were a child?
• Did you eat a lot of junk food when you were a child?
• Is TV important in your life nowadays?

Format: Large Group/Whole Class

Culture and Alcoholism

At a university in the U.S., some international students were asked to talk about the attitude toward alcohol in their cultures. The students who participated were from France, Argentina, Japan, Russia, and one Arab country.

According to the French student, the French drink a glass of wine with almost every meal. For her, alcohol is an everyday part of life, even from a young age. French parents teach their children about alcohol. They believe a glass of red wine every day is good for you. The French student also explained that people don't drink in order to get drunk, but rather, they drink to be sociable. Furthermore, they feel that drinking wine during meals helps them enjoy the taste of their food more. Because the French start drinking at an early age, they don't think of it as being an adult activity; therefore, most young people don't abuse alcohol. However, if someone develops a problem with alcohol in France, they can easily find a free clinic that will help them.

The woman from Argentina said that in her country also most people drink to be sociable. There are few traffic accidents as a result of alcohol, because most people feel a responsibility to be careful when they drink too much. For example, they usually walk or take a bus if they feel drunk.

The Japanese student said that Japan doesn't have very strict drinking laws. He said that it's easy for young people to get alcohol, so there are often problems with alcohol abuse. In Japan, alcohol is sold in vending machines; this means that even children can buy it! According to this student, there are many accidents in Japan caused by drunk drivers. One cause of the problem is that companies often organize drinking parties after work, so workers feel pressure to drink.

When asked about his country, the Russian student looked very sad. Drinking is a great problem in his country, he said softly,

Unit 33 is continued on the next page.

Nine Discussion Choices

and nobody knows what to do about it. The government talks about solutions, but no one takes the talk seriously. This problem has deep roots in the culture and the history of Russia, the student added, and it will only change when great changes come to the life of the average Russian.

Finally, the Arab student talked about alcohol in her country. Since hers is a Muslim country, alcohol is strictly forbidden. Simply put, it's against the law to sell or drink alcohol, and it is against the religion. It is true that some people do buy alcohol on the black market. However, since most people obey the law, there's no problem with alcohol abuse.

Factual Questions about the article

1. _____
2. _____
3. _____
4. _____
5. _____

Reaction Questions about your opinions and experiences
(You can write your own questions and/or choose some of these.)

• Are the drinking customs in the U.S. and your country the same?
• What does alcohol mean to you?
    a) relaxation
    b) feeling happy
    c) celebration
    d) forget your problems
    e) a waste of time and money
    f) something unhealthy
    g) something evil
    h) other
• Some teenagers in the U.S. drink alcohol because they want to be like adults. Do teenagers in your country do things to be like adults?

Format: Large Group/Whole Class

Boredom

Researchers visited some prisons and interviewed a variety of prisoners. They wanted to find out why these prisoners had committed crimes. The researchers found that one of the biggest reasons was because the criminals were bored. In other words, they committed crimes in order to relieve their boredom.

Boredom is similar to hunger. If we feel hungry, it is a sign that we need food. If we feel bored, it is a sign that we need some physical or mental activity.

Thousands of years ago, people probably didn't get bored because they were too busy. They spent most of their time looking for food or growing it, as farmers. In the Middle Ages, about a thousand years ago, some people became rich, so they didn't need to work as farmers. And they had extra time when they had no work to do. In order to not get bored, they learned how to read and write books, play music, create art and dance.

Recently, technology has caused some problems that are connected to boredom. For example, some people are very good at using computers. So when they get bored, they use their computer skills to send a virus to other computers.

Also, technology has created many new types of jobs. Several years ago, before there were any computers, many jobs were too difficult for women because they required workers who were very physically strong to do them. As a result, often women stayed at home and had time to teach their children games and other ways to not feel boredom. But because of technology, these days, there are a lot of jobs that are perfect for women. So there are not so many women who spend all day at home and take care of children. As a result, children are not learning (from their mothers) how to stay busy.

A third connection between technology and boredom is about TV and video games. Often, these activities don't require much

Unit 34 is continued on the next page.

mental energy. In other words, we don't have to think very hard to use them. They are less challenging (mentally) than reading, card games and puzzles. Therefore, people will feel bored more quickly when they watch TV or play video games.

Recently, schools spend most of students' time on classes that will help them when they look for jobs. For example, schools focus on math, science and computer technology. And they spend less time on teaching leisure skills. "Leisure skills" are activities that we can do when we are not working. In fact, some schools are dropping subjects like music, art, drama and dance. This causes a problem for these students. In the future, they might not have skills that they can use during their free time that will keep them from becoming bored.

In conclusion, it's important for our schools to realize that students need both work skills and leisure skills. Everyone is happier when they are not bored, and some people even commit crimes because they are bored, which is not good for society.

Factual Questions about the article

1. _____
2. _____
3. _____
4. _____
5. _____

Reaction Questions about your opinions and experiences
(You can write your own questions and/or choose some of these.)

- Do you ever get bored?
- Do high schools in your country teach students leisure skills, like music, art, drama and dancing?
- Do you enjoy leisure skills, such as playing a musical instrument, painting, dancing, or writing poems?
- The article says that video games do not require much mental energy. Do you agree? Do you sometimes get bored when you play those kinds of games?

Format: Large Group/Whole Class

Keys to Happiness

This article is about happiness. It seems that there are some factors that can make people happy.

One factor is money. Money can make us happy, but after we have enough money to pay for our food, clothes and a home, extra money doesn't make us a lot happier.

Another one is charity. Charity means helping people by giving money or doing nice things for them. Studies have found a connection between charity and happiness. However, we are not sure whether doing something good makes people feel happy, or whether happy people are more likely to do good things.

A third factor is friendship. A researcher interviewed very poor people in India who lived in the slums of Calcutta. He found that they were almost as happy as middle-class students in that city. He explained the possible reason for this. Apparently, these slum-dwellers have a strong social support system. This means that they have many relatives, friends, and neighbors who help each other.

Age is another key to happiness. In one study, researchers compared people between the ages of 18 and 94. They found that old people experienced as many positive feelings every day as young people. However, old people also experienced less negative emotion than young people. Why are old people happier? Scientists say that perhaps older people know that life can be difficult, so they are more realistic about their goals, and there is a smaller chance that they will be disappointed. Also, they know that they might not live many more years, so they focus on things that make them happy, for example, a beautiful sunset, or a good dinner, or the sound of birds that are singing.

Unit 35 is continued on the next page.

Some people believe that intelligence would make a person happier because smart people tend to make more money. Surprisingly, there seems to be no connection between intelligence and happiness. Researchers believe that extremely intelligent people expect to have high achievements. However, often, their expectations are unrealistic. As a result, they are unable to achieve everything that they want, and in the end, they feel disappointed. Also, a person who can get a good score on a test, which means he knows a lot of information, might not understand how to get along with other people, which is also an important key to happiness.

Factual Questions about the article

1. _____
2. _____
3. _____
4. _____
5. _____

Reaction Questions about your opinions and experiences
(You can write your own questions and/or choose some of these.)

• Do you agree that money is not an important key to happiness?
• Do you know someone who seems very happy? Can you explain the reasons why they seem happy?
• When do you usually feel especially happy?

Nine Discussion Choices

Format: Large Group/Whole Class

The Clown
and the Cell Phones

Researchers at Western Washington University, in Bellingham, Washington, did some research about people who were talking on cell phones. They wanted to know if a person who is talking on a cell phone will notice unusual things around them. For the experiment, a man put on a clown suit. The suit had a lot of bright colors. Also, he wore big red shoes and a red nose. Then, he got on a unicycle, which is like a bicycle but has only one wheel. He rode the unicycle around a big central square in the middle of the campus.

After some students walked around the square, the researchers asked them this question: Did you see anything unusual in the square?

Here are the results of the research:

- Among students who were walking with a friend, nearly 60% said that they had seen the clown.

- Among students who were walking alone or listening to music on headphones, 30% said that they had seen the clown.

- But among students who were talking on a cell phone, only 8 % said that they had seen the clown.

The researchers then asked some students this question: Did you see a clown on a unicycle in the square?

Here are those results:

- Among students who were talking with a friend, 71% noticed the clown.

- But among students who were talking on a cell phone, only 25% noticed the clown.

Unit 36 is continued on the next page.

Nine Discussion Choices

Factual Questions about the article

1. _____
2. _____
3. _____
4. _____
5. _____

Reaction Questions about your opinions and experiences
(You can write your own questions and/or choose some of these.)

- Do you think that you would notice the clown if you were talking on your cell phone?
- Have you had any experiences that were dangerous while you or someone else was talking on a cell phone?
- If you have a cell phone, how would you feel if you couldn't use it for a week?
- When other people are talking on their cell phones, do they sometimes bother you?

Format: Large Group/Whole Class

Family Meals

When you were a high school student, did you eat dinner with your family? While you were eating dinner, did you watch TV?

Some people think that watching TV while eating dinner is bad for the relationships of a family, so researchers studied this topic. They looked at two types of families: families who watched TV during meals and families who did not. According to the results, the children who did not watch TV did eat healthier food, but in general, the differences between the two types of families were small. The researchers found that the most important factor was just that the families ate together. In other words, if a family ate meals together, the children ate more healthy food, whether the TV was on or the TV was off.

Researchers found that kids who eat meals with their parents usually eat more fruits and vegetables, and they get more vitamins and eat less junk food. Also, these types of kids are less likely to smoke, take drugs or drink alcohol.

The researchers studied 5,000 middle school and high school students in the U.S. About 66% of the students said that they ate dinner with their parents at least three times a week. About half of those students said that their family watched TV during dinner.

In addition, the study found that girls who ate dinner alone ate fewer fruits and vegetables and drank more soft drinks and ate more snack food than girls who ate with their families. Also, girls who ate with their parents ate more calories. In fact, they ate 14% more calories, which is good because calories are important for their physical development.

Unit 37 is continued on the next page.

Nine Discussion Choices

Surprisingly, researchers said that having the TV on during dinner might actually have a positive effect. Some teenagers prefer to not eat with their family members. They would rather eat alone in their bedrooms, where they can watch TV, use the internet or talk to friends on the phone while eating. As a result, if a family has the TV on during dinner, the kids are more likely to join the parents at the dinner table.

Another reason why eating dinner together is good is that it is a nice time for a family to talk. Nowadays, people are busy and have little time to spend together. So if a family can eat together, the parents have a chance to talk to their kids about their school life and about their friends. Also, the parents have a chance to just look at their children in order to see if they have any problems.

In sum, there are many benefits to eating meals together as a family. And it doesn't matter if the TV is on or off.

Factual Questions about the article

1. _____
2. _____
3. _____
4. _____
5. _____

Reaction Questions about your opinions and experiences
(You can write your own questions and/or choose some of these.)

- When you eat dinner with your family, do you watch TV?
- Do you think teenagers in your country like to eat meals with their parents?
- In general, do teenagers in your country eat healthy food?
- When you eat meals with your family, what do you talk about?

Format: Large Group/Whole Class

International Students in the U.S.

Two 17-year-olds discussed their experiences as international students in the U.S. The students, from Brazil and France, had studied at a high school in Wisconsin.

Poliana came from Brazil to the U.S. for academic reasons. She wanted to improve her English, because it could help her get a better job, maybe even a job teaching English someday. She's interested in traveling and studying different cultures. She said that Brazilians try to copy North American customs, so she was interested in understanding why.

Before coming to the U.S., Poliana had a certain image of North Americans. She got her image of North Americans from watching North American TV and movies in Brazil. She saw several Hollywood movies about high schools in the U.S., and she imagined high school could be a lot of fun. High school students seemed to have a lot of freedom. She imagined they participated in a lot of fun activities both inside and outside of school. However, she now thinks that Brazilian students have more fun and freedom in school.

Poliana sometimes feels disappointed because outside of school there are few places for young people to meet their friends and talk. In Brazil, young people often get together at parties or at a shopping mall.

In addition, Poliana thinks most North American students pretend to like her, because she comes from a foreign country, but actually don't make an effort to get to know her well. She also feels North American students often discriminate against other students who don't have fashionable clothes and hairstyles. In her opinion, North Americans aren't open to different cultures and customs.

On the other hand, Poliana says she likes North American ice cream, horses, and fashions.

The second student, Caroline, comes from France. The things she likes the most about North America are her host family, cheeseburgers, and peanut butter.

Unit 38 is continued on the next page.

Nine Discussion Choices

Like Poliana, before coming to North America, Caroline had some images of what she expected. She imagined that there would be a lot of freedom and that North America would have many things that she couldn't find in France. She believed in a stereotype. She was sure North Americans would all be wonderful, attractive, and very intelligent. After arriving, she found out she'd been wrong. And, unfortunately, to make matters worse, many North Americans seemed uncomfortable with her when they found out that she was French.

Caroline has noticed two big differences between North American and French young people. First, she thinks it's strange that people under 21 can't drink alcohol, as they can in France. And second, it seems all U.S. teenagers dress in the same style of clothes. In France, there's a greater variety of fashions.

These were the observations that two international students made about their experiences living and going to school in a small North American town.

Factual Questions about the article

1. _____
2. _____
3. _____
4. _____
5. _____

Reaction Questions about your opinions and experiences
(You can write your own questions and/or choose some of these.)

• Before you met any Americans, what image did you have of them? Did your image change after you met some?
• Have you visited any other countries? Were the countries or people different from what you had imagined before going?
• What three countries would you like to live in for a year?
• In general, how do people in your country treat foreigners who visit or live there?

Format: Large Group/Whole Class

Students' Choice
Designing and Leading Discussions

Preparation steps

(1) Find an article that you think would be interesting for the other students in the class. The article can be in your native language or in English.

(2) Tell your teacher the general topic of the article. Each student should have a different article and topic.

(3) Write a summary of the main idea of your article with some interesting details. This will be the basis for the discussion.

(4) Write *Factual Questions* about the article and some *Reaction Questions* asking about your partners' opinions and experiences.

(5) Your teacher will schedule you to be the leader of a discussion and tell you if you will lead a whole-class or a large-group discussion. Your teacher will set the discussion time for 20, 30, or 40 minutes.

When you're the discussion leader

1. Give your summary to the group and use **discussion strategies** (e.g., ask them if they understand, answer their clarification questions, explain words they do not understand, and ask other participants to help you explain ideas.)

2. Ask your *Factual Questions.*

3. Ask your *Reaction Questions,* and use **discussion strategies** (e.g., ask follow-up questions, and ask for more details.)

When you're a member of a discussion group

Try to be an active member by using **discussion strategies** (e.g., ask clarification questions, answer with details, ask other participants follow-up questions, volunteer answers, clarify by summarizing, and help the leader explain words and ideas.)

Instructions for the Students

Suggestions to the Teacher

General

Why these activities were developed

A complaint often heard from both ESOL and subject-matter instructors is that their international students are passive in group and whole-class discussions. At the same time, international students tell us that they're quiet because they feel they don't know what to say, they don't feel they have anything interesting to say, or they have difficulty understanding what others say but are embarrassed to admit it. Furthermore, they may say they come from cultures where spontaneous give-and-take interaction in class isn't valued (or is even discouraged), and they don't know the "rules" for participating in this kind of interaction. This text is designed to better prepare international students to interact in discussions.

The approach and sequence

The units are presented with detailed instructions, so that the role of the teacher, after getting the students started, becomes that of supporter and coach. The students develop their skills and confidence by practicing with each other. The sequence of units leads from relatively easy challenges to the ultimate goal of leading and participating in a large group discussion, and therefore, as the later units build on earlier ones, the units are intended to be done in the order presented.

It should also be noted that the group format for the units leads, in general, from pair and triad work to large group and whole-class work. This approach is another reason for following the units in order.

In the event that your class doesn't divide easily into pairs or triads, two students can work together as a team carrying out the "Student A" role. For example, let's say you have 20 students and the unit calls for triads. You set up six groups of three, and then have each of the remaining two students team up with one of the students who has been assigned the role of "Student A."

Suggestions continued

Setting up discussion groups

There are various ways to form the pairs, triads, and groups. Some teachers may feel most comfortable taking on the role of match-maker. With specific classes, depending on the mix of personalities or other cultural considerations, it may be important to assign students to groups carefully, with an eye toward balancing the challenge and comfort that each student needs. An extremely shy and hesitant student probably should not be assigned to a triad with two other students who are aggressively eager to express themselves. When getting started with this book, some match-making should be considered if the style of these discussion activities is new to the students. Initially working in comfortable groups will help all the students gain confidence quickly.

On the other hand, random matching can easily be justified, since the activities are designed to turn taciturn students into active participants and talkative dominators into willing turn-takers. Another benefit of random matching is that the reorganizing and rearranging of groups, day after day, creates situations in which the students, in fact, need to draw upon the various strategies introduced in the text to interact with partners of varied personalities and abilities. Thus, by the end of the course, students will be experienced at working with other students who are more extroverted and more introverted, as well as others more and less fluent than themselves.

Getting started

Especially with Unit One, and even with some of the later units, it is important to be sure the students understand how the units are structured. Therefore, it can be helpful to choose a Student A and B team and walk them through the directions as the others observe, to show everyone how the activity works.

Students should be told to focus their attention on their assigned roles as Student A or B, etc., and not look at their partners' pages. "Cheating" spoils both the discussion and the fun.

Extending the activities

After some groups have (almost) finished the activity, ask everyone to stop. At this point, if there is time and the students seem involved and willing to extend the activity, you can invent ways of extending it. Here are two recommended options. You can ask everyone to switch parts, form new groups, and start over with just the *Reaction Question* discussions. Having changed the composition of the groups should make it more interesting to go back over the *Reaction Questions*. Or you can have the students discuss the *Reaction Questions* as a whole class.

Evaluating

Another important role that you as the teacher could play is as facilitator when the students evaluate their own and their group's performance and progress. The class as a whole can spend the final five minutes of class on "discussing the discussion." You may want to supplement this by providing individual students with some on-going feedback.

On page 220, following the notes on specific units, there is an evaluation form. How you use it is up to you. You could fill one out for each student, although this is difficult since you have several discussions going at once. You could focus on one or two students each day and give them a filled-out form as the basis for a brief one-on-one feedback session. Alternatively, you could have the students use the form for a self-evaluation or to evaluate their partners. Evaluations can be made after a certain number of classes or after specific units; the discussions in Units 6, 10 or 11, 14, 17, 21, 24, and 28, which summarize preceding lessons, offer appropriate occasions for evaluation. Whatever form or format you use, it is important to help the students assess themselves on an on-going basis, so that they see their own skill development and progress, two important aspects of developing confidence and expertise.

Dealing with early finishers

If you find that a group has finished the activity far in advance of the others, they could be offered three choices: a. switch parts and rediscuss the *Reaction Questions*, b. discuss any topic they like in English, or c. just take a rest and say nothing.

Suggestions continued

Special notes on specific units

Unit 1 and all of the following units provide your students with questions that are intended to stimulate discussion. Many of the questions ask students to share their personal opinions and experiences. This makes even the controlled discussions "real." However, a student may not be able to answer a question because it assumes they have had an experience they haven't had. This problem may embarrass them and make the whole discussion awkward for everyone. You may anticipate this problem by teaching the class this strategy. "What do you say if a question doesn't apply? Politely say you don't know or can't say, and give some explanation. For example: *A: Do you have to work hard in college? B: I'm sorry, I don't know. I'm still in high school.*"

Unit 3 is the first unit to use the news article topics, and for that reason, you may want to be sure that the students understand that they are to read the articles carefully enough so that they can discuss them in detail. Inevitably, they will encounter new words as they read; although vocabulary development is not the focus for this material, it may be important to allow them time enough to look up definitions or ask for help so that they will feel confident enough to discuss the topic. At any rate, you should provide some guidance on understanding the passage.

Unit 6 is the first "discussion unit," so you may want to be sure the students understand the purpose of the unit. In this case, as with later discussion units, they should attempt to put into use the strategies they have been practicing in the preceding units. In Unit 6, for example, they should be making a conscious effort to use the strategies of Units 1-5: rejoinders, asking follow-up questions, asking for clarification, providing comprehension checks, and answering with details.

Unit 16 has a unique set of directions involving a "small group" of five students. (If necessary, the groups can be four or six students.) Once again, be sure that the groups understand the directions for the activity. You may want to choose one team of five to "walk through" the directions while others observe how the activity works.

Unit 28 is a special summary unit in which all the strategies are reviewed and practiced. This unit includes a list of performance indicators, so it can be used to evaluate the students' progress in learning the basic discussion strategies. Videotaping one or more of the triads could provide a useful follow-up to this summary unit.

Unit 29 is a teacher-led unit, although you could have one or two of the more confident students take on the leadership role. This is the first "large group/whole class" unit, so if you model the role of the leader, the students can focus on participating as members, while at the same time observing your style as a whole class discussion leader.

Units 30-39 are large group/whole class discussions, in which the students have the opportunity to lead a discussion on their own. Although you could let the students choose which discussion topic they prefer, please note that the readings in these units progress in length with Unit 30 being the shortest. Keeping this in mind, you may want to assign the shorter passages to students who work more slowly and the longer ones to those who work quickly or who want more challenge.

The teacher's role

Throughout the book, once students have begun a unit there is usually little need for further teacher input. However, an effective use of your time is to roam among the groups, listening to the discussions and noting those who are doing well and those who are not. This information can allow you to provide additional guidance, support, and encouragement when they are needed and recognition and praise when they are warranted.

Note: On the next page there is a form that can be used for giving each student an individual evaluation. It is photocopyable.

Name _____
Date _____
Unit(s) _____

Discussion Evaluation

I heard you: **I didn't hear you:**

_____   Use rejoinders   _____

_____   Ask follow-up questions   _____

_____   Ask for clarification   _____

_____   Use comprehension checks   _____

_____   Answer with details   _____

_____   Interrupt someone   _____
                   appropriately

_____   Re-tell information   _____

_____   Volunteer an answer   _____

_____   Re-tell others' opinions   _____

_____   Help the leader   _____

_____   Express an opinion   _____

_____   Refer to a source   _____

As a discussion leader:

You seemed to be _____ prepared.
   a) very well   b) well   c) somewhat   d) not

You _____ tried to get all the members to speak.
   a) often   b) sometimes   c) rarely

You _____ explained well if a member didn't understand.
   a) often   b) sometimes   c) rarely

You _____ asked follow-up questions about members' answers.
   a) often   b) sometimes   c) rarely

I think you should work on _____.